SATURATION

A STRATEGY
FOR GOSPEL IMMERSION

DAVID BEIDEL

Printed in the United States of America.

Cover design by Jan Hamilton Art & Design.

Second Edition, Printed January 2016
ISBN 9781519509529

I'd like to dedicate this book to my beautiful wife of 25 years.

You, my love, are the delight and joy of my life. Whatever path the Lord has taken on, whether through meadows of wonder or through the valley of the shadow of death, your hand always reached for mine, and your heart has always chosen love and faithfulness. You have always been by my side and on my side. I could never thank you or love you enough.

By the river by the sea, in the land of grace and glory
You and me, face to face with our Beloved crying "Holy"
All our stains washed away, all our trials turned to gold
Side by side in the garden of the Lord.

Side by side in the garden of the Lord

WHAT PEOPLE ARE SAYING ABOUT SATURATION:

Hours after arriving on Staten Island as a new ministry leader Pastor Dave Beidel invited me to a weekly clergy prayer meeting. I could hardly believe my good fortune! I had no idea I would find more than just a prayer circle! I discovered a group of leaders passionate for Jesus and desperate to make an impact for the Kingdom of Jesus—Together! Under Dave's leadership the churches of Staten Island have united to form a beautifully connected church—truly the way church should be. This book will inspire you take steps in your local context to form the connected and collaboratively minded church that your community desperately needs. **– Lt. Stephen Mayes, Salvation Army**

David Beidel gets it. We become answers to Jesus' prayer -- and the prayers of others -- and advance Jesus' kingdom "on earth as it is in heaven," when we demonstrate the Gospel, not just talk about it. This book offers a framework for believers to practice tangibly what we preach rhetorically in ways that impact real people where they live, work, and go to school every day. **– Jeremy Del Rio, Esq., Thrive Collective**

With his book, Saturation, David Beidel accomplishes something of great value to the 21st Century church. He offers church leaders a concrete, step-by-step blueprint for empowering their congregations to fulfill the Great Commission on every level: Individual to individual, church to individual, and church to community. Drawn from what he learned through his church's mobilization across Staten Island in the aftermath of Superstorm Sandy, Beidel goes beyond the platitudes and clichés we know so well. The wisdom found in this book is hard-earned through experience. And that experience has shown Beidel a model that works. Readers of Saturation will see a clear path – one modeled in both the Old and New testaments – to build their churches into pillars of light within their communities and beyond. **– Dr. Mike Scales, President, NYACK College and Alliance Theological Seminary**

In this short, powerfully written book, David Beidel teaches us how to pastor a city. From his own depth of pastoral experience on Staten Island, he shares stories and metaphors that illustrate a clear and compelling vision for the many blessings God longs to unleash locally through love, prayer, and the hard sought unity of pastors and church members. His vision is for the "house of the Lord" to experience God's glory, God's tangible presence to such an extent that it spills over through the hands, hearts, and voices of His people transforming the community, the city, and the entire world. **– Dr. Glenn Barth, Author of** THE GOOD CITY**; President, GoodCities Ministries**

Saturation is more than a good idea, it is truly a desire of many of our pastors and leaders in Staten Island. David Beidel's passion to see the church united for Gospel and Kingdom saturation is expressed in his life and leadership. His efforts to gather the body of Christ together for collective ministry is equaled by his desire for Christ alone to be made known and glorified. **– Tim McIntyre, Oasis Church**

Where life is most raw, the church must be the most real. In times of need and crisis there is no time to 'play church.' Saturation is an unusual combination of inspiration and story,along with a practical plan to continually impact a geographic area with the attractive love and light of the Gospel. David Beidel shows us what the church at its best can be. Outstanding book. May the Lord give it wings." **– Eric Swanson, Leadership Network, Co-author of To Transform a City: Whole Church, Whole Gospel, Whole City**

I have been a privileged witness of Dave's vision for a unied church to love, serve, and share the good news every day- in their schools, in housing projects, and on the streets. The result is clear- dozens of Staten Island churches are leading the way in a united, holistic, and sustainable ministry that blesses their neighborhoods and their cities. This is exactly what the church needs! **– Kevin Palau, President, Luis Palau Ministries**

Saturation has one of the greatest prayer and action strategies I have witnessed. Pastor David has a great plan for cities around the country to implement. **– Dimas Salaberrios, President, Concerts of Prayer of Greater New York**

Pastor David Beidel presents an effective and enduring plan to reach our communities. Saturation focuses on building relationships in the community as the catalyst for change. As an elected official, I have been around many "campaigns" which seek to reach out to the communities they are seeking to influence. But in this book, outreach is taken to the next level where the needs of the community are met as an effective way to saturate our neighborhoods with the gospel. I strongly encourage every pastor and leader to implement this strategic approach as a concerted effort to win regions and whole territories for God. **– Dr. Fernando Cabrera, New York City Councilmember**

CONTENTS

ACKNOWLEDGEMENTS 9

FOREWORD *by Mac Pier*. 11

INTRODUCTION. 13

CHAPTER ONE: Great Commission Contractors. 19

CHAPTER TWO: The Acts 1:8 Plan 27

CHAPTER THREE: Acts 1:8 Start-Up. 49

CHAPTER FOUR: "I Did Not Come to Make Business". 63

CHAPTER FIVE: A Tale of Three Temples 79

CHAPTER SIX: Living Stones 91

CHAPTER SEVEN: Sweet Hour of Prayer. 97

CHAPTER EIGHT: In My Father's House. 107

CONCLUSION 113

ABOUT THE AUTHOR 117

ACKNOWLEDGEMENTS

I would like to thank Rev. John Saldanha for his encouragement and support during the writing of this book.

Thank you to Dr. Mac Pier and Mark Giacobbe for their counsel, Mike Avaltroni for formatting the e-book, and to Deborah Feeney and Kathryn Sarcone for their editing and assistance throughout this project.

Many thanks to the amazing pastors that I serve with on Staten Island. What an honor it has been.

I would also like to thank the thousands of volunteers that "out flooded" Hurricane Sandy and brought healing and blessing to our people.

FOREWORD

David Bryant, the father of the modern prayer movement, has said that "revival is the approximation of the consummation." His words echo those of Habakkuk, "For the earth will be filled with the knowledge of the glory of the Lord as the waters cover the sea" (Habakkuk 2:14).

Dave Beidel's book, *Saturation*, echoes that vision. As God has brought the nations of the world into the neighborhoods of our cities, we are witnessing an unprecedented opportunity. The opportunity is to creatively and intelligently mobilize the body of Christ city-by-city and block-by-block to saturate our cities with the glory of God. The best way to do that is through united prayer and outreach in the streets of our cities.

We are learning from our thirty years of experience in New York City that when leaders are more present to each other, then God becomes more present to the city. *Saturation* is really a manual on how to foster this kind of presence to each other through united prayer.

Hurricane Sandy is a metaphor for the challenges our cities and neighborhoods face. Every city faces enormous pathologies – poverty, fatherlessness, low graduation rates, unemployment, and incarceration. Our cities and communities are battered by challenges that are overwhelming in the natural.

Dave Beidel provides a model of the ways churches can work together to make a measurable impact on their communities. Dave has been a practitioner for decades in some of the toughest neighborhoods in New York City. His model and vision will inspire you and your church to act. The only difference between where you are today and where God wants you to be a year from now is the commitment to lead. Saturation provides a simple guidebook on how to lead in your church and in your community.

Dr. Mac Pier

CEO and Founder, The NYC Leadership Center

Senior Associate for Cities, The Lausanne Movement

September 2015

INTRODUCTION

sat-u-rate (verb)

1. Cause (something) to become thoroughly soaked with liquid so that no more can be absorbed.

2. To cover a city and/or region with the knowledge of the Lord as the waters cover the sea.

In October 2012, Superstorm Sandy hit New York City. It was a natural disaster beyond any we had experienced in recent memory in the Northeast. Staten Island, where most of my ministry is based, had the most extensive damage and the greatest loss of life of any area affected by the storm. Twenty-four people died, and over twenty thousand homes were damaged. Nearly seventy thousand people were displaced or rendered homeless in one night.

Pastor Tim McIntyre, my dear friend and the sitting president of our regional pastors' association at that time, lived and served at the storm's "ground zero." Both his home and his church, Oasis Christian Church, had been swamped by the deadly surge of water. The morning after the storm, members from nearly a dozen local churches converged at his doorstep, ready for action. Within twenty-four hours, his church had become a literal "oasis" in the midst of the devastation, opening its doors as a neighborhood relief center.

Donations of clothing, toiletries, and food were dropped off by the truckload in the church's small yard. Volunteers seemed to come from everywhere. Pallets of bottled water, diapers, canned goods, and clothing filled the sidewalk and the upper level of Oasis Christian Center. However, by the end of the week, Tim began refusing supplies and turning away volunteers.

Would-be Good Samaritans swarmed his neighborhood, directionless. Countless contractor bags full of used clothes and various supplies began to clog Tim's church yard. We quickly found ourselves floundering in the murky waters where "helping hurts." This was truly tragic, because there was no lack of crisis. There were thousands of under-served neighborhoods that desperately needed assistance, but there was no infrastructure in place to assess the rapidly changing needs of those affected by the storm.

With no central agency to allocate volunteers and distribute resources, the influx of supplies and helping hands couldn't be used efficiently. To further complicate the matter, it was a challenge to accomplish anything because many major roads were still under water, and the devastation covered the entire eastern shore of our borough.

It was in the midst of this frustrating conundrum that forty local pastors and ministry leaders gathered to pray and plan.

PARISH PARADIGM

The Staten Island Association of Evangelicals (SIAE) has had its share of challenges and personality struggles, yet it's members have also established many rich, long-term friendships. Six months prior to "Sandy," several churches in the association had begun serving together in the style of a parish model. Six different churches each adopted a different housing project on Staten Island. We pooled our resources, shared best practices and strategies, but served different ministry communities.

We quickly realized that incorporating a similar parish paradigm was the only way that all of us could effectively serve our traumatized borough in the aftermath of the storm. On the night of our first post-Sandy meeting, we created seven parishes, each comprising between twenty and thirty square blocks. We designated three types of churches in our coalition: Parish Churches, Hub Churches, and Support churches.

The Parish Churches became the boots-on-the-ground, face-to-face, door-to-door expression of the body of Christ. These churches took on the responsibility of visiting every home, assessing the need for human and material resources. They also provided orientation, training, and direction for the tens of thousands of amazing volunteers that were streaming in from all over the country. This ground-level engagement enabled us to determine accurately which resources, tools, and survival necessities were most needed.

Hub Churches received, warehoused, and delivered large shipments of construction necessities, tools, food, and water. Large groups of volunteers could also meet there, and then be transported to the parish that needed manpower.

The Support Churches were able to provide special services according to their abilities. Some delivered food to storm victims and volunteers; some provided medical or legal assistance; others, laundry services -- and so forth.

Within four months, our coalition had collectively visited nearly every home in every parish we had established.

Together we identified the neediest, prayed with the distressed, and served thousands of households. Together we facilitated and gave direction to over twelve thousand volunteers, mucked out and gutted nearly fifteen hundred homes, and distributed several million dollars in food, supplies, and tools. Together we organized a spring beautification campaign six months after the storm. Once again, hundreds of volunteers served tirelessly on Easter weekend, repairing torn-up lawns and restoring storm-trampled gardens. One of our new friends simply said, "Everything was so ugly. But then you came again, and restored our hope."

A crowning, God-kissed event came on the anniversary of the storm. Four hundred members from all the different participating churches hosted a "Day of Hope" festival and evangelistic outreach. Over a thousand people came from the flood zone. These were our new friends with whom we had prayed, cried, and served for over a year. As we welcomed all those gathered to call on the name of Jesus to be saved, it seemed every voice joyfully cried out to the Savior they had encountered all year long.

Jesus was not a stranger in this community. His people had made Him known. His people had made His praise glorious. We prayed that this Saturday in late October would be remembered as the most beautiful day of the year. It was.

Many of us continue to this day to rebuild homes. We continue to reach out to the most vulnerable and helpless within the flood zone. In these hard-hit communities, you will hear testimony after testimony of how "the Christians" rescued them in their darkest hour.

A HOLY FLOOD

A dream arose from the ashes of Hurricane Sandy. We tasted of John 17 during those days in a way we never had before. A unified army of saints from Staten Island and volunteers from around the nation effectively ministered to nearly every nook and cranny of our storm-traumatized neighborhoods. We saw a partial fulfillment of the great dream of God: that His glory would cover the earth as the waters cover the sea.

Together, we began to dream of Kingdom saturation: a unified church in Staten Island serving together, supporting one another, creating synergy and exponential impact. We had experienced a kind of solidarity with Nehemiah as each of us took our place on the wall and worked in unity to rebuild our ruined city. We saw the power and effectiveness of brotherly love combined with an agreed-upon strategic plan.

So many walls came down after the storm; walls that should never have been there in the first place. In spite of the overwhelming crisis, amazing victory was seen. We couldn't help but think about the words of Christ, "I will build My Church, and the gates of hell will not prevail against it" (Matthew 6:18).

This devastating flood did not prevail against the Church of Staten Island in 2012. From the saltwater wilderness that the Atlantic Ocean left behind, there was a blossoming. It was as if a tender sapling of the true Church that Jesus came to build arose from Sandy's wake. We tasted the first fruits of His House – and now, we hunger for much more.

CHAPTER ONE
GREAT COMMISSION CONTRACTORS

It was one of my last conversations with Arthur DeCesario, the father of a dear friend. He was eighty-three years old, and ill at the time. I was fascinated as he began to tell me of the house that his own father had built.

Vito DeCesario was an Italian immigrant, a cement worker who lived and worked in Manhattan in the early 1900s. After many years of hard labor, while supporting a family of six, he managed to save enough money to buy a small plot of land on Staten Island.

He traveled every weekend by ferry to his property, where he left a shovel and a wheelbarrow. Weekend after weekend over the next several years, he dug and laid a cement foundation, built thick cement walls, framed and covered the roof, laid out the plumbing and electricity, and cultivated an enormous garden on the unclaimed land behind his plot.

Finally, the day that he had dreamed about for more than twenty years came. He brought his family into their own home, built by his own hands. I never met Vito DeCesario, but to this day I am moved by hunger to build a home.

Christians come from a long line of builders: Moses, Solomon, and Jesus, the carpenter from Nazareth. The word "carpenter" in the New Testament text actually means "builder." Very little is said about these twenty-some years of Jesus's life, but when we consider that redemptive history centers around three construction projects, his life-long trade cannot be dismissed. We call these construction projects "the Tabernacle" and "the Temple," but God fondly referred to each building as "the House of the Lord."

Moses built the Tabernacle in the wilderness; then Solomon built the Temple in Jerusalem. The third Temple was built by Christ Himself and continues expanding as He reigns in and through us. Paul explains that we are "built on the foundation of the apostles and prophets, Christ Jesus himself being the cornerstone, in whom the whole structure, being joined together, grows into a holy temple in the Lord" (Ephesians 2:20, 21). In other words, believers are a temple built by Christ himself.

We don't often use literal building terms when we discuss the New Testament Church, but it is "constructive" for us to think like architects and general contractors. When someone is building a church, a school, or a shopping mall, there is a great deal of activity. Many laborers, sub-contractors and materials are needed. If there is not an overall plan and a general contractor directing the entire project, it is doomed. Half a dozen sub-contractors wouldn't even attempt to build a small house without an agreed upon blueprint and action plan. Yet today, millions of saints and thousands of ministries are feverishly working to build God's kingdom with neither.

Something our coalition of pastors discovered in the aftermath of Sandy was our desperate need for structure. We needed a coordinated action plan. It was wonderful that we cared for and spoke well of each other, but there is a great difference between emotional and functional unity. The crisis at hand was not an abstract concept. It was labor-intensive and messy.

We needed to coordinate the allocation of professional contractors, weekend warriors, youth groups, shovels, crow bars, wheelbarrows and hammers. Desperate families were counting on us to send well-equipped and capable teams of volunteers to muck out their homes. Salt water and sewage destroyed or contaminated the entire contents of homes. Soaked sheetrock and wood floors had to be gutted and removed before black mold set in.

> We became "contractor pastors." As it turned out, we were very good shepherds when we thought like contractors!

Then there was the spiritual fallout from the disaster, as damaging as the loss of property. We needed to assign our more sensitive servants to pray and cry with the frail and elderly as they sifted through their precious few salvageable items. The hands-on, vast and visceral need forced us to operate as many sub-contractors, co-laboring on an enormous project.

We became "contractor pastors." As it turned out, we were very good shepherds when we thought like contractors! We were excellent collaborators when the options were to: a) work together or b) epically fail.

Our experience raised the question, "What if we operated like contractor pastors as a way of life?" What if we began to approach our Great Commission as our New Covenant Temple construction project? It's not much of a stretch given the overarching Temple building narrative of the Bible. The new perspective has helped our fellowship, and we pray it will benefit you and your city.

STRUCTURE AND SPIRIT

The building and rebuilding of the Lord's house has been the main event of every Biblical era. Each great movement in Biblical history culminated in the establishment of a Holy house in our unholy world. Although our New Covenant building project utilizes living stones instead of dead ones and the entirety of the earth is our building plot, we are still builder/priests or "contractor/pastors."

In all my years of preaching, I never saw a connection between the Old Covenant "great commissions" given to Moses and Solomon, and our New Covenant Great Commission. It also puzzled me that something as vast and vital as "The Great Commission" could be driven mainly through one short scripture reference: Matthew 28:19-20. It seems that this final charge of Christ should be more fully nuanced and strategically empowered.

However, when the Great Commission is viewed as the final Temple construction project, fascinating Old Covenant/New Covenant parallels come into view. The nuance and strategy are there; they color the story of the Old and New Testament and produce a stunning blueprint for believers.

Just as the sacrificial system of the Old Covenant deepens and enriches our understanding of Jesus as, "the Lamb of God," the building of the Lord's House can deepen and enrich our understanding of our calling to reach and disciple all nations.

One of the most important concepts to ponder as we explore this parallel regards the dual roles that Moses and Solomon played in the story of the nation of Israel. Each had two responsibilities: 1. Build the Lord's House; 2. Build up the priestly tribe. They had blueprints for building the Lord's House and manuals for training and equipping the priests. They built their structures and trained the priesthood according to the specifications they were given. Their commission had both spiritual and structural components.

If they had only built a structure, the Lord's house would have been empty. If they had only trained a priesthood, the Levites would not have had a house within which to fulfill their calling. Both commissions were vital. We the Church have also been given a dual roles in our New Covenant Temple building commission. We must build up a holy priesthood and we must erect a holy Temple. This temple is not made of wood and stone, it is comprised entirely of living stones. The Temple/Church is intended to cover and fill the entire earth. We are "His body, the fullness of him who fills all in all." (Eph 1:23).

It is unreasonable to think that God would not provide a different kind of blueprint for this different kind of temple. We must surmise that for such an ambitious building project, the blueprints would be easy to find; most likely in the first chapter of the book of Acts. In addition, given that the entire structure is comprised of living stones, these blueprints would encourage the wise deployment and allocation of human resources. Finally, there would be a clear safeguard embedded in the blueprints that would ensure that strategically minded persons would constantly need to acknowledge that it is "Not by might, nor by power, but by my Spirit says the Lord."

For these and many other reasons, I am convinced that the Acts

> Just as the sacrificial system of the Old Covenant deepens and enriches our understanding of Jesus as, "the Lamb of God," the building of the Lord's House can deepen and enrich our understanding of our calling to reach and disciple all nations

1:8 Great Commission is a God given, powerful blueprint for coordinated and comprehensive, city saturating and earth encompassing
ministry.

For centuries the Church has mainly concerned itself with the
"Spiritual/Levitical" aspects of her calling. By neglecting to ponder
or establish a few basic structural components, she has greatly compromised her health, limited her advance and limited her capacity to
make mature disciples.

Although never perfect, and some might say woefully inadequate,
every Christ-centered church in the world has invested most (if not
all) of their efforts into fulfilling their mandate to raise up a kingdom
of priests. Our evangelism, discipleship, education and leadership
development endeavors can all be categorized as the Levitical facets of the "New Covenant Temple." But rarely do ministries ponder
or invest in the big-picture architectural strategic implications and
admonitions of the New Testament.

Nearly all of my own preaching and teaching has been imbal-
anced thusly towards discipleship. Even when I touched on the
structural admonitions expressed in the New Testament, my teaching was disconnected from the whole, similar to a contractor foolishly
constructing a bedroom, or bathroom that is not incorporated into a
home.

This is a Catch-22 scenario. Ministries invest countless hours
in discipleship, only to agonize over the sparse returns. Much of the
frustration regarding discipleship may be related to this disconnect.
If the Levites did not have a structure through which to perform their
duties, all the training in the world would have been in vain. If we are
structurally unsound, then we are consistently undermining our own
disciples.

Structural soundness in construction mainly requires three

things: First, an agreed upon blueprint; next, solid "building blocks" or building materials, and thirdly, the "glue," or binding components that hold everything together. The Church requires the same. Throughout the remainder of the book, I will refer to these three components.

In the next two chapters we will explore the merits of employing the Acts 1:8 Great Commission as a blueprint for our New Covenant Temple construction endeavors. In Chapter 5, "A Tale of Three Temples," I explore the great Temple meta-narrative in more depth. For those of you who are intrigued by the New Covenant Temple concepts introduced in this chapter, I would recommend reading Chapter 5 next. The entire book is based upon the confidence that God has provided us with a viable strategic plan for building His holy temple. For those of you who appreciate seeing strategy up-front, please continue the chapters in sequence.

DISCUSSION AND REFLECTION QUESTIONS

1. List each time in Scripture the House of the Lord was built, rebuilt or restored.

2. What were the events that led up to each "main event"?

3. How significant were the outcomes?

4. What are some insights we could glean from these building projects that might help the Christ honoring churches in your region "grow into a holy temple in the Lord." (Ephesians 2:21)?

5. How do you think you might become more like Jesus the carpenter/builder if you were to think more like a contractor building the House of the Lord in your community or city?

CHAPTER TWO

THE ACTS 1:8 PLAN

For the earth will be filled with the knowledge of the glory of the
LORD as the waters cover the sea.

Habakkuk 2:14

In the past, reading this verse from Habakkuk would evoke images of an enormous, luminous cloud rolling over nations and continents. Yet the New Testament paints a less dramatic picture for us. Instead of a great fiery cloud, we see tax collectors, healed demoniacs, and fishermen flooding their communities with the good news of God's glory come down. While studying the impact of the early church, historian Michael Green discovered the same pattern; it was primarily the "informal missionaries" -- the peasants, merchants, servants and washwomen that spread the Gospel throughout the known world.[1]

You and I and the rag-tag team called "the Church" are the principal conduits of God's glory.

The image that pops up in my mind now when I think about God's glory covering the earth, is that of my son painstakingly spreading butter on his English muffin, making sure to fill every nook and cranny. This is the calling of the Church: to ensure that every nook and cranny, every dark place, every forgotten neighborhood,

---

1   Michael Green, *Evangelism in the Early Church* (Grand Rapids, Mich.: Wm. B. Eerdmans Publishing Co, 2004), 17.

and every fractured family is engaged and infiltrated by the glorious people of God.

The Habakkuk passage is repeated three times in the Old Testament. The larger sentiment of God's Kingdom advancing, reaching out and filling the earth permeates both the Old and New Testament. I believe Acts 1:8 to be the strategic expression of God's beautiful vision. In one brief sentence, the Lord laid out a simple, flexible, culturally and geographically transcendent, strategic plan to cover the earth with His glory as the waters cover the seas.

But you will receive power when the Holy Spirit has come upon you, and you will be my witnesses in Jerusalem and in all Judea and Samaria, and to the end of the earth.

Acts 1:8

Before Luke had even penned these words, the fledgling New Testament Church was honoring this command. Within a decade, the saints had saturated Jerusalem, Judea, and Samaria with "rivers of living water." Many had already begun to reach out in every direction to bring the Gospel to the ends of the earth. We can broadly distinguish the Great Commission of Matthew 28:18-20 as the more Levitical/Spiritual admonition and the Acts 1:8 Great Commission as the "blueprint/strategic plan."

Throughout the history of the church, mission-minded saints have contextualized Acts 1:8 in order to operate strategically in new regions. Since we are declared to be "living stones," it makes sense that our New Covenant temple blueprint incorporates the wise allocation of human resources. Acts 1:8 effectively deploys believers to spread the word of God throughout any given area. In our context, it has become a practical template for strategically mobilizing our people and coordinating outreach.

As evangelists throughout the centuries brought the Gospel to new frontiers, Jerusalem was generally understood to be the most influential city, or the area surrounding the mission base. Judea was seen as the region, or nation. Samaria was often interpreted to represent communities of ethnic minorities or disdained persons within or immediately adjacent to "their Judea." The ends of the earth clearly represented surrounding cities and nations.

A vital task for all true churches in a given region is to contextualize Acts 1:8. This can be as simple as gathering a critical mass of Christian Leaders for prayer and writing on a large white board, "Jerusalem, Judea, Samaria, the ends of the earth – how are we to fulfill our purpose to be His witnesses for our generation?" There will be many different nuances in the resulting outreach strategy. From state to state and nation to nation, unique approaches will arise. However, the final product will be a plan to saturate every nook and cranny of the given region with the full expression of the Gospel.

I recently took on the miserable task of painting the exterior of my eighty-five-year-old home. I love building, but I hate painting. In the past ten years I built a deck, two sheds, put in a pool and built a screen house for my wife. All during this time I have known that my house needed painting. Truth be told, I almost let my house go too far. Neglecting to seal the house was foolish.

The problems with the protective skin of my home were far greater that I had imagined. From the street view, my house looked "okay." From my ladder, it was in terrible disrepair. I was horrified at what I discovered as I engaged in the tedious work of scraping old paint, caulking holes and repairing rotting wood (No, I can't afford vinyl siding). Thank God a good friend brought his sprayer and helped me cover a lot of square footage, but now that he's done, I am left with brush and roller in hand to finish the work.

In many ways my construction preferences parallel my ministry preferences. I love new, big projects, but I have learned over and over again that without tedious and consistent shepherding of the flock and neighborhood, the house of the Lord can fall into disrepair. Without the personal touch, we can easily lose touch with the real battles going on in our community.

Sometimes we can use "sprayers" such as mass media and crusades to cover a lot of territory in a short span, but if we don't take the time to fill holes and deal with the rotten patches of our cities, our efforts will ultimately be in vain.

When we get up close and personal, what we thought to be a peaceful neighborhood may not be as idyllic as we imagined. In my city, a heroin epidemic has broken out in the area that was considered to be an upper middle class, family-friendly community. It came as a great surprise to us. From the street view, everything was "okay." Up close it is a nightmare.

Sometimes we can use "sprayers" such as mass media and crusades to cover a lot of territory in a short span, but if we don't take the time to fill holes and deal with the rotten patches of our cities, our efforts will ultimately be in vain. Can we say that on our watch, we have saturated our region with "the knowledge of the glory of the Lord as the waters cover the sea?" This is impossible without a coordinated cooperative plan.

We need to work together with the big spray guns and we need to pick up the two-inch finish brush to care for the more complex, intricate and hard-to-reach families and individuals. Otherwise, our work will be shoddy, incomplete and ineffective.

SATURATION FROM THE TOP DOWN

Our association of churches in Staten Island is seeking to walk together as an Acts 1:8 City. Our goal is to "reach every one, and disciple every willing." Nothing about this is quick and easy, but we know that it is the Great Commission we are entrusted with : to build the Lord's House in our city. Here is the quadrilateral plan that is guiding our current outreach and several steps that are being taken.

Jerusalem: ZIP CODE

All participating ministries have identified the ZIP code of their physical locations as their Jerusalem. As simple as this may seem, it has enabled us to focus our evangelism, follow up, and discipleship endeavors to ensure 100 percent coverage. Our goal is to ensure that every person in every ZIP code in Staten Island is prayed for, visited, blessed, and evangelized within the next two years.

As we strategically map every block and plan outreaches with our immediate community in mind, we are seeking to keep tight records of who has been visited, who is receptive, and who is in need of assistance. We want to know, for instance, where the elderly, the widows, and single mothers are in our community so that we can be sensitive to their physical needs. We want to know where there might be drug trade and gang activity so that we can pray with insight. We want to follow up on those who show an interest in learning more about Jesus or being discipled.

This kind of deep ministry is impossible without the establishment of wise boundaries. We are developing a shared parish model in which churches adopt a portion of their ZIP code as their area of Gospel and prayer responsibility. For example, sixty-six thousand people live within my church's ZIP code. Within that same area, there are several Christ-centered churches. We have created a grid in which each church is taking responsibility for part of its ZIP code in order to ensure full Kingdom coverage. We emphasize consistently, however, that no neighborhood belongs to any church. This is not about territorialism; only saturation. This parish/visitation model was carved into our souls as we engaged in relief ministry following Hurricane Sandy.

Strategic door-to-door visitation is not an original idea. Jesus practically commanded it in Luke 14:16-23. Unfortunately, the Mormons are currently the most dedicated to this command. They have mapped cities and strategically visited homes for decades. During this time, evangelicals have shied away from door-to-door ministry. Interestingly, a recent Census study has shown that "in the nine most populated metropolitan areas...Evangelical Christians increased their numbers by 12.3 percent and Latter-day Saints increased their numbers by 66.9 percent."[2]

If the evangelicals in the nine largest American cities grew at 66.9 percent, we would be in the midst of the greatest revival in our nation's history. There are other factors, but it is not an overstatement to say that we are rapidly losing ground because we have abandoned door-to-door engagement.

I have heard it said many times: "We don't want to be associated with the Jehovah's Witnesses or the Mormons." With that statement,

2. "Religion Census: Increase in Evangelicals, Mormons; Decrease in Catholics, Mainline Protestants." http://www.christianpost.com/news/religion-census-increase-in-evangelicals-mormons-muslims-decrease-in-catholics-mainline-protestants-74207/#eowWxjBmJ6lo6sEZ.99. Accessed April 2015.

we surrender Jerusalem. We bemoan the slowness of the Lord to send revival, yet we disobey Him. Jesus stands at the door and knocks, we should too. The Mormons are experiencing a revival devoid of the Holy Spirit. In the following parable, we see a direct challenge to saturate our streets with the good news.

> But he said to him, "A man once gave a great banquet and invited many. And at the time for the banquet he sent his servant to say to those who had been invited, 'Come, for everything is now ready.' But they all alike began to make excuses. The first said to him, 'I have bought a field, and I must go out and see it. Please have me excused.' And another said, 'I have bought five yoke of oxen, and I go to examine them. Please have me excused.' And another said, 'I have married a wife, and therefore I cannot come.' So the servant came and reported these things to his master. Then the master of the house became angry and said to his servant, 'Go out quickly to the streets and lanes of the city, and bring in the poor and crippled and blind and lame.' And the servant said, 'Sir, what you commanded has been done, and still there is room.' And the master said to the servant, 'Go out to the highways and hedges and compel people to come in, that my house may be filled.'"

Luke 14:16-23

Judea: PUBLIC SCHOOLS

For our Judea commission, we are identifying several regional cross-sections of our borough. Our leading question is, "In what ways can we serve and reach our region better collaboratively, rather than separately?" For our first collective initiative we are focusing on our public schools. We are encouraging each church to come along side one school through prayer and acts of kindness. I understand this is easier dreamed than done.

If you are like me, you may at times feel like you are one straw away from a broken back. When Jeremy Del Rio, a passionate advocate for the NYC Public Schools, challenged me to partner with a nearby school, I hedged initially. I shared with him that since we have been devoting so much energy into reaching out to our neighboring housing project, the thought of spreading our efforts to minister to our local elementary school was overwhelming. Undeterred, he enthusiastically shared with me his passion for public school ministry. He craftily convinced me that I was a lesser member of the Kingdom of God if I ignored the plight of our NYC schools. Finally I relented and asked, "Okay, how do we start?"

His reply was simple. "Reach out to the school's principal and let them know you would like to be a blessing to the school. Maybe do a community clean-up or plant a garden. See if they would like to be involved in a mural project. Maybe have a teacher appreciation breakfast or donate some school supplies."

So, in the spring, we approached the principal and asked if we could be of assistance to the school. I mentioned an opportunity we had to plant a community garden for them. His eyes lit up as he told me that a beloved teacher who had served in the school for over 30 years had passed away recently. They had planned to build a memorial garden for her, but didn't have the financial or human resources. From the get-go we were perceived as a "God-send" and an answer to prayer.

The memorial garden was a smashing success. Our church's after-school program children and youth group, the principal, several teachers, a local garden club, and many children from the school joined us on a beautiful Saturday in May to plant a gorgeous garden. The entire school could not have been more grateful.

In fall of 2014, we invited the teachers to our church for a teacher's appreciation luncheon. The principal brought seventy-five of his teachers and staff, including security guards. We blessed, thanked, and prayed for the teachers. Some cried, and all were overjoyed to be cared for and appreciated. We understood our need to be politically correct. There was no overt Gospel message, but a gift packet of Christian literature and music was made available. Nearly everyone took a packet.

We told the principal about the potential for a mural project. He said he would love to see that happen. We are seeking a grant at this time to realize this goal. In October of last year, we received a donation of daffodil bulbs which we planted in several places, including our beloved elementary school. Again, our kids and children from the school joined together to plant these wonderful fall bulbs.

During the bulb planting, the principal told me that the Department of Education had forbidden them to use their school kitchen to cook for their annual Family Thanksgiving Dinner. He asked me apologetically if we might consider hosting the dinner. We said, "Of course; we would be honored." The next week, however, the school called to cancel the event because of budgetary problems. We reached out to Lt. Steven Mayes of the Salvation Army for help. He has been a wonderful partner in our pastor's alliance. He graciously contributed twenty-five turkeys and a total of $1,000 in food. We had the sweetest Thanksgiving party in West Brighton with our congregants, the principal, teachers, parents, and students all feasting and celebrating together.

We are in awe of what God has done in such a short period of time. Not every engagement will be this sweet and easy, but this harvest is so plentiful. Several of our churches on Staten Island are now partnering with schools, praying for schools, assisting with school supplies, and helping with backpack giveaways. Several were already doing so, but now a comprehensive movement is taking shape.

Last year we were able to bring in several Christian NBA players to speak to students in nearly a dozen schools. We keep discovering that wherever we plant our feet, God gives us the land.

There are several other Judea or "regional cross-section" ministries that we are engaging in or discussing. We have expanded the scope of our Hurricane Relief Teams to include caring well for our "widows and orphans in distress" (James 1:27). This amazing construction ministry which is headed up by Pastor Tom Basile has also been a wonderful place to train some of our floundering youth. We

> We have observed repeatedly that whenever a church puts down its feet in these neighborhoods, there is a reduction in murders committed and the healing of generational brokenness begins.

have been able to prepare them for work and connect them with gainful employment opportunities.

We are currently bringing together our Kingdom marketplace leaders for mutual encouragement, support and to help us work on employment solutions for our borough. We also want to do a better job praying and caring for our boroughs first responders, including police, firefighters, and EMTs.

Samaria: HOUSING PROJECTS

For our Samaria commission, we are seeking to adopt all of our housing projects and blighted communities. In cities throughout our nation, these communities in particular are in desperate need of long-term, sacrificial ministry. Over a dozen churches and several para-church ministries are now engaged in ministry to our eleven housing projects. These blighted communities are adopted through prayer, prayer evangelism, consistent visitation, acts of kindness, children's ministry, and various community outreaches.

Like a small seed that takes root invisibly and later blossoms beautifully, we are joyfully watching ministries in these challenging neighborhoods bear great fruit. Satan has thrived in these neighborhoods because in the past, many churches walked away. He seems to put up a sign that says, "GO AWAY, YOU ARE NOT WELCOME HERE." Unfortunately, too many nod at Satan and say, "Yes, sir." We have observed repeatedly that whenever a church puts down its feet in these neighborhoods, the murder rate declines and community healing begins. In our own neighborhood, the murder rate has declined 95 percent over the past sixteen years.

When we purchased our broken-down warehouse in the middle of West Brighton, a.k.a. Bloody Brighton, our neighborhood was traumatized by seventeen murders every year. In obedience to the Lord's direction, we fasted corporately and prayed against the murders in West Brighton. God brought peace in response. The challenges are many, but the presence of God is more powerful. We constantly feel God's favor as we reach out to these troubled communities.

During a Pastor's prayer meeting, Rev. Steve Martino shared about a new initiative to begin a comprehensive sports outreach in an abandoned athletic field next to the South Beach housing projects. After Pastor Steve approached him, our Borough President allocated $15,000 to fix the fields and help launch the program. In addition, one of the managers from the housing community gave Pastor Steve a room full of sports equipment.

Through our recent partnership with the Luis Palau Association, over the past six months we were able to minister powerfully to thousands in or next to seven local housing projects. There was food, music, literature, children's books, athletic events, and plenty of fun for all. It was glorious. Hundreds responded to the Gospel.

In NYC, the 334 public housing communities provide an obvious parallel to Samaria. Some contexts are not as clear. In my book *Samaria: The Great Omission*, I deal with this subject in greater detail, but here is the abbreviated version to identifying your Samaria.

What neighborhood do fathers tell their wives and children to avoid? "Don't ever drive through _____" That's your Samaria. The Jews in the day of Christ circumvented Samaria. It is wise to exercise utmost caution, as many of these areas are dangerous. However, the Church cannot circumvent these oppressed communities, as they are filled with the broken-hearted and "the least of these."

What neighborhood in your region is the butt of most racial slurs? The Jews in the day of Christ called the Samaritans "dogs."

What community in your region is characterized by multi-generational devastation? Samaria had been trampled on for over 600 years when Jesus met the woman at the well. She had been married 5 times and was living with a man. So the scriptural clues help us to see an area of cultural and personal brokenness, religious confusion and moral decay.

Is this community within a two or three hour drive of your church? Samaria was next door to Judea but "across the tracks." This is important because the key to transformation in these troubled neighborhoods is consistent, long-term spiritual and relational investment. This is unsustainable if the community you wish to serve is several hours away.

Sometimes the best way to "adopt a Samaria" is to come alongside a ministry that is already there. Churches like mine that serve in broken neighborhoods are often overwhelmed, understaffed and exhausted. We cherish partnerships from surrounding communities.

A beautiful relationship has been developing between our church and Stonecrest Community Church, a church in suburban New Jersey. Their partnership with us over the last two years has been an incredible blessing, and life-saving in a multitude of ways.

Many people come to our shores from nations where just communicating with a Christian could have dire consequences.

The freedom to dialogue with and befriend followers of Christ is unprecedented for these individuals.

In addition to our public housing focus, our Samaria initiative is addressing our current drug abuse epidemic and the hidden nightmares of human trafficking and domestic violence. To these and other Samarias, we must be the first responders to the cries of these who have been devastated for generations.

The Ends of the Earth: ETHNIC ENCLAVES

All of our churches are currently involved in overseas mission work. This is the apparent and vital admonition of reaching out to "the ends of the earth." However at a local level, we are seeking to capitalize on the amazing opportunity that all major cities have: the nations of the world have come and are coming to us.

For instance, in NYC, nearly 800 different languages are spoken and over 35 percent of the population is foreign-born. This puts us in a unique position to serve, befriend, and evangelize immigrants and internationals. Through the wonderful website/ministry "EthNYCity," major ethnic enclaves in each of the fifty-nine community districts of NYC can be identified.

Our association of churches has recently identified the large ethnic groups in each of our community districts and is preparing to strategically address the need. This will help us to wisely allocate our efforts to ensure that we are evangelizing the nations in our own backyard.

Many people come to our shores from nations where just communicating with a Christian could have dire consequences. The freedom to dialogue with and befriend followers of Christ is unprecedented for these individuals. We have become more intentional about educating and empowering our people to reach the nations by reaching out to community members from places such as India and Tajikistan.

My wife and I met Daniel Chintimalla at a gas station half a mile from our church. As a recent immigrant from India, he worked long hours to survive here while supporting his family back home. We befriended him and prayed with him for nearly a year before he was able to convince his boss to give him Sunday mornings off. He began attending our Church faithfully. Soon he invited his brothers to attend. We discipled him and he discipled others. After a few years, he began a Telagu speaking congregation in our Church.

We prayed for many years that his wife and two children would receive visas in order to reunite his family. It became clear, however, that the Lord had different plans. God called Daniel back to Hyderabad, India to be a minister of the Gospel. Now nine years later, his church is rapidly expanding and he is bringing together pastors in Hyderabad to saturate their city with the Gospel through an Acts 1:8 model.

It was my privilege to minister side-by-side with him as we shared the beautiful Gospel with hundreds of villagers and untouchables in Shadnagar and Hyderabad, India. He is preparing to launch a collaborative work that has the potential to reach thousands of villages in the forests outside the city proper. Most of these villagers have never heard the name of Jesus.

Another couple in our church are Uzbek and Kazak. They constantly share with me wonderful testimonies of family members and business associates in the most closed nations on earth, receiving Christ in Skype and phone conversations. They have also been tutoring and evangelizing Central Asians through ESL classes for several years. Many Muslims and atheists from Tajikistan, the Ukraine and Uzbekistan have been saved. They in turn share the Gospel with their families here and abroad.

It has been fascinating to observe how swiftly the Lord is building His House in our city. It is as if we were all disconnected "tongue-in-groove" components of a modular building project.

The ends of the earth came to Staten Island, and now they, in turn, reach out to the ends of the earth.

PRAYER RHYTHM

One simple pattern that keeps us marching in sync is what we call an Acts 1:8 Prayer Rhythm. Every first week of the month many of our churches pray corporately for Jerusalem. The second week, Judea; the third, Samaria and the fourth, the ends of the earth. It has been fascinating to see how quickly the Lord has responded to our prayer and unity. Within a very short period of time, we have experienced supernatural favor in our schools, neighborhoods, and housing projects. In 2014 and 2015 alone, the collective impact of our collaborative and strategically-coordinated ministry has impacted over twenty-five thousand unchurched Staten Island residents!

It has been fascinating to observe how swiftly the Lord is building His House in our city. It is as if we were all disconnected "tongue-in-groove" components of a modular building project. After we laid a foundation, churches, parachurches, movements, and ministries all began to find their footing and a place to interlock. We have also found that very little needs to be invented. Each of our churches and parachurches all contained unique strengths and gifts. The greater need was for interconnectedness. As we shared our treasures with each other, a glorious edifice began to rise.

Tim Keller has often beautifully expounded upon the word "shalom" as the weaving and meshing together of a community that results in "full flourishing." This has been our experience. The weaving has gone far beyond the walls of our own borough.

As Staten Island began to experience a level of synchronicity, it became easier to plug in vital and powerful ministries that served in the greater metropolitan region. There are hidden treasures in every city that God has planted with excited expectation for a glorious John 17 day.

For instance, Concerts of Prayer Greater NYC (COPGNYC) has been promoting PRAY NY for nearly a decade. This wonderful initiative calls for all New York Christians to prayer walk every street in every ZIP code of the five boroughs. As you can see, the Jerusalem component was already in place. NYC has been prepared for such a time as this. We are working together with COPGNYC to transform

THE ACTS 1:8 PLAN

this amazing day into an amazing year-long movement.

Two great young men of God in our city, Jeremy Del Rio of 20/20 Vision and Paul Coty of Young Life, have been impacting schools and connecting churches with schools for the last ten years. Much of what we have done in Staten Island to reach out to our schools, we learned from them. This Judea component was easily incorporated into our collective outreach.

A dear friend in the Bronx, Rev. Que English, has developed a powerful movement for combating Human Trafficking and Domestic Violence called "Not on My Watch." This Samaria component has been pre-built. Our association of pastors welcomed this treasure and now we are ready to engage in rescuing the captive and the oppressed as we network with this well-established movement.

Many pastors who have ministered in the NYC housing projects are fully committed to assisting churches and church planters to reach these challenging communities. We readily share strategic plans, ministry ideas and resources with anyone who desires to be involved in this ministry.

Nearly a million people dwell in the 334 housing projects of NYC. Over two hundred thousand single mothers are struggling to raise their children in some of the most adverse conditions imaginable. This is a work that requires the full expression of the body of Christ.

In his book, *The E-Myth Revisited*, Michael Gerber reveals that over 80 percent of independent small businesses fail within ten years.[3] Church plants have a similar success rate. However, franchises succeed at a 75 percent rate within the same time frame. He explains that franchises provide a support team, a manual, a prototype and a

3. Michael Gerber,. *The E-Myth Revisited* (New York: HarperCollins, 1995), 83.

proven strategy. We are attempting to build these systems for those that come to labor in our city.

In their highly celebrated article, "Collective Impact," John Kania and Mark Kramer propose the following:

> *Substantially greater progress could be made in alleviating many of our most serious and complex social problems, if non-profits, government, businesses and the public were brought together around a common agenda to create collective impact. It doesn't happen often, not because it is impossible, but because it is so rarely attempted. Funders and non-profits alike overlook the potential for collective impact because they are used to focusing on independent action as the primary vehicle for social change."* [4]

Very few organizations on earth have the capacity to orchestrate "collective impact." The Church is the most capable because of its altruistic and collaboratively-oriented doctrines, its enormous human resources and capacity for multi-generational longevity. Yet, we often fall into the same trap of focusing on independent action. Although our doctrine orients us towards collaboration, our habits and history orient us toward isolation. We could easily provide manuals, prototypes, strategy and team support for start-ups, but this, tragically, is a rare scenario.

What could happen in our cities if church planters and city mission outreaches were blessed and buttressed by the existing body of Christ? What if local churches pitched in strategically to help with the incubation of new ministries? What if sharing strategies, resources, and support systems were the normal mode of operation across our

---

4. John Kania and Mark Kramer. "Collective Impact," *Stanford Social Innovation Review* (Winter 2011.)

THE ACTS 1:8 PLAN   45

nation? We must dream these dreams of God for our cities.

SATURATION FROM THE GROUND UP

Charismatic leaders and local churches are like the Air Force: they are very important, but without ground troops going door-to-door, no lasting victory is won and no territory retained. The most powerful ministers of the Gospel have always been friends and neighbors, co-workers and business associates. Every follower of Christ has been assigned a unique niche and corner of this world to shine into. There is no grand strategic initiative that will ever prosper without grass roots engagement.

> Charismatic leaders and local churches are like the Air Force: they are very important, but without ground troops going door-to-door, no lasting victory is won and no territory retained.

As stated earlier, our overall goal is kingdom saturation: "to reach every one and disciple every willing." No strategic plan can bear fruit without friend-to-friend and neighbor-to-neighbor engagement. Water covers the sea deep and wide. Only family, friends, neighbors, and coworkers can go deep. For these reasons, we are encouraging not only local churches, but every believer to adopt an Acts 1:8 lifestyle.

In a celebrity-enamored culture like ours, it is easy to fall into the trap of believing that sharing the Gospel should be left up to the professionals, the talented, and the scholars. This attitude undermines and enfeebles the potency and purpose of Pentecost. The explosive growth of the Early Church far beyond the borders of the Roman Empire can only be attributed to a massive "lay movement," empowered by the Holy Spirit. Thousands of nameless and faceless unprofessionals and unknown heroes of the faith filled the earth with the Gospel (*The Spreading Flame*, F.F. Bruce[5]). The priesthood of believers is the greatest army on the earth. We have a sacred responsibility as pastors and leaders to lead this army well.

For four centuries, the New Testament Church experienced explosive world-transforming growth. From its inception in Jerusalem the "little flock" reached out, saturated the entire Roman Empire, and continued to expand far beyond her borders. In order to saturate our city from the ground up, we are encouraging and enabling all of our congregants to pray for and reach out to their neighborhoods as their Jerusalem. As their grass roots Judea assignment we are asking them to reach out where they work, shop and go to school. To reach their Samaria, we are asking that they open their eyes to the rejected, troubled and disdained in their midst. For the ends of the earth, we are training and empowering our people to evangelize the internationals and immigrants among us and then assisting them to reach their friends and family in their homeland.

As dozens of churches align themselves strategically through an Acts 1:8 Plan, and our saints engage their neighborhoods through a parallel model at a grassroots level, we are beginning to taste the first fruits of true "shalom." We are seeing the knitting and weaving together of the Body of Christ. We are excited and overjoyed to operate in this fashion, we see the potential for true kingdom saturation and awakening in our city.

I often think of Kevlar when I contemplate the beautiful and powerful tapestry of God's kingdom. Not only is Kevlar an incredibly strong plastic, it is tightly wound and woven together, making

---

5. F.F. Bruce, *The Spreading Flame* (Eugene, OR.: Wipf and Stock, 2004), 337..

this lightweight material capable of stopping a bullet. May we see the day when the Church is so powerfully and intricately woven together that the bullets of addiction, violence, human trafficking and abuse are rendered impotent in our towns and cities. When the Church of a city or region is unraveled, the bullets of the enemy are far more devastating. We must be knitted and woven together, He in us, us in Him, we in one another, that the world might know Him and that Eden might arise for these ashes.

MAPPING EXERCISE:

A. : If you are doing this exercise as a leader or leadership group within a local church:

1. Draw a map of your zip code or a cluster of zip codes in your church's vicinity.

2. Then outline what you feel best represents your Church's "Jerusalem."

… Samaria (Samarias are not always within the "city limits," if so indicate this in your map)

…Ends of the earth (ethnic enclaves, sometimes Samaria's and local ethnic enclaves are one and the same)

4. Then fill in the map by drawing in other churches, schools and significant businesses in the area.

5. Spend some time praying over each aspect of your map.

B. If you are doing this as part of a coalition of pastors:

1. Draw a map of your region (Judea).

2. Begin to draw the different churches represented at the table.

3. Add churches that you feel would be willing to partner in an evangelistic coalition.

4. Identify the schools, Police, Fire Stations and EMT's.

5. Identify the Samarias of your area, low income/subsidized housing, trailer parks, Indian reservations...etc.

6. Pray over and believe God to saturate every nook and cranny of your region with the glory of God. Keep praying till you have possessed your city by faith.

CHAPTER THREE
ACTS 1:8 START-UP

This chapter lays out a framework containing simple, practical steps that a small or large coalition of churches can take to build up a more strategically aligned Church in any city.

CLARIFY KINGDOM BOUNDARIES

There is a clear sense of territory and boundary established in both Testaments. Each of the twelve tribes of Israel were responsible for self-care; however, the nation operated as one in worship, celebration and warfare.

Similarly, the New Testament supports the concept of boundaries. There are numerous clear city church delineations throughout the New Testament. In the epistles and the letters of Christ to the seven churches in Revelation, each addressed a city church: Philadelphia, Ephesus, Rome, Corinth, and so on.

Many of these city churches were in close proximity to each other, yet they were understood to be distinct entities. Most of these cities were between five thousand and two hundred thousand in population. Putting these factors together helps us to envision boundaries for sustainable church cohesion.

For instance, New York City is home to over eight million people. It has been described as the "city of a thousand cities." Gathering weekly and establishing meaningful relationship with thousands of pastors is impossible. Paul Coty, metro director of Young Life, has developed an excellent strategic approach to this challenge. He has proposed that we identify the fifty-nine Community Districts (CD) of NYC as "distinct cities." Each CD has a population between 35,000 and 250,000, and these regions have their own cultural vibes and political representatives.

This is a wise and Biblical approach that is building momentum in New York City. Our current goal is to identify "shepherds" over every CD that will in turn identify ZIP code shepherds. Together they will be responsible for bringing together the Christ-centered pastors and churches in their district for prayer, good works, and gospel saturation.

These shepherds are easily identified. For years they have been calling together pastors for prayer. They, like Barnabas of the New Testament, reconcile brothers and are always working for the common good. They are beloved by most and know to be "good shepherds." I have found that it takes very little time to find these humble leaders. As soon as I mention, "we are looking for Barnabas types in this community," a few pastors will smile and nod as this individual is brought to mind. These shepherds will be asked to champion a loosely structured movement of unified prayer and strategic outreach in their district.

Incorporating a loose organizational structure is crucial. Most of us have organizational ties. The goal is fostering prayer, communication and strategic cooperation on the streets of the communities that we serve. Even the loosest organizational structure that is able to facilitate broad communication and coordination within clearly delineated boundaries, will have amazing impact.

All cities and communities in every nation have unique boundaries of this sort. Clarifying these zones will enable focused

collaborative ministry. Indigenous leaders will best determine these
ministry districts.

BUILD KINGDOM POWER

Every city and community on earth has hidden treasures. If one
looks hard enough, they will find passionate marketplace believers,
like-minded politicians, lay leaders who quietly minister to their
communities and little parish churches that are poor and few in number but are the healing nexus of a blighted neighborhood. Parachurch
organizations are also powerful allies in our cities. They often focus
on a particular need or population and become experts at meeting
that need. Finding, mapping and partnering with these and many
other hidden jewels is a vital step towards community transformation.

This is the boiler room from which all the heat and power flows:
the simple weekly prayer meeting of one to two hours a week. In
our gathering, sometimes only five pastors attend. Sometimes it is
twenty-five. The "sweet hour of prayer" gathering to which we have
committed has done more to build unity and oneness of spirit than
any project, crusade, or big city event.

We have discovered that trying to pull off a huge crusade or
multi-church evangelistic event without the foundation of consistent
prayer and relationship-building often ends in frustration and division. In the best of scenarios, a large event brings churches together,
but following the event there is not enough genuine relationship to
retain oneness of spirit.

Isaiah 49:8-9 tells us to "reassign the desolate inheritances" and
to say to those in captivity, "Come out!"

This is our privilege as joint heirs of Christ: to lay claim to areas
that Satan has called his own. We first win these regions in prayer.

Like an air force dominating the skies, our prayers clear the way for our ground troops to rescue the captives and occupy the wastelands. As we obey Christ's command to abide in Him and love one another, we are confident to "ask whatever we wish." We are confident to call forth cities and nations in Christ's name.

As we pray, we also humbly acknowledge that "we are powerless against this great horde that is coming against us. We do not know what to do, but our eyes are on you," (II Chronicles 20:12). As we pray we realize that we all have feet of clay, we all have family struggles, and we all need someone to pray with that understands the unique challenges of our position.

When you really pray with brothers and sisters, hearts are wide open and trust follows. I cannot overemphasize this first step. Please don't take on any initiatives until you have prayed together for at least six months.

ASSESS KINGDOM POTENTIAL

Parachurch ministries love to work with our association because we are not territorial. They are designed to operate at the regional level, so networking and partnering with us flows naturally and rapidly. Business leaders and politicians as well appreciate the broader scope of concern and the community cohesion that we are able to inspire.

We work together with many powerful ministries and parachurch organizations. We are proud to network and/or partner with: Metro World Child, Child Evangelism Fellowship, Times Square Church, Calvary Baptist Church, the Bowery Mission, Young Life, ENGAGE and Seekers (High School Campus Ministries), Convoy of Hope, God Belongs in My City, Luis Palau Association (LPA), 20/20 Vision,

City to City, the Salvation Army, Urban Impact, CRU NYC, Ignite, Not on My Watch, and a host of visiting church groups.

We find that church mission teams also love working with us because there is always something meaningful to do. If, for instance, one church has a team that it cannot well utilize for a full week, a member will call another from our association and share the blessing.

BUILD KINGDOM SYNERGY

We are always trying to imagine how ministries can have exponential impact through wise collaboration. When all the players are at the same table, it's exciting to dream about all the possibilities. It just takes prayer, humility, creativity, and time to build synergistic relationships. Once they are in place, the impact is exponential for each entity and the entire community.

For example, Pastor Ray Parascando has been doing a great job mobilizing volunteers to paint local schools for several summers. Now, however, whenever he paints a school, he asks me who in our coalition is caring for that particular school. Even though he organizes everything and does 90 percent of the work, when he is done, he gives the sweat equity of the relationship he has earned with the school administration to the partnering church. How good and pleasant it is when brothers dwell together in unity (Psalm 133:1).

At a certain point in our city, the most divisive component was the church calendar. We all cared about one another and had a great desire to work together, but coordinating our calendars was nearly impossible. This takes a while to overcome and needs a great deal of intentionality and flexibility.

Through our weekly meetings and our constant attempt to provide services that will bless our entire borough, we are learning to plan further in advance, synchronize our calendars more effectively, and pace our big events in such a way that we ensure maximum involvement.

INITIATE KINGDOM SATURATION

A simple exercise to get moving is to create an Acts 1:8 Ideal Scene. Plan a half-day retreat with the regional leadership team and on a large whiteboard write: IDEAL SCENE. Then create four sections labeled: Jerusalem, Judea, Samaria and The Ends of the Earth. Pray and dream over the vital ministry targets in each sector. As you dream of God's kingdom transforming each ministry population, write down what you see. This is your ideal scene. For instance, one ideal scene for Staten Island as it regards outreach to our public schools is to facilitate partnerships between all of our churches and schools. Another ideal scene is to provide 2nd and 3rd Grade reading assistance to our poorest elementary schools.

Start with the dream, envision it clearly, write it down and possess it by faith. Begin with faith filled prayers, broad strokes and big dreams. Don't allow doubt to poison this prayerful, joyful process. Sometimes, specific visions and ideas will arise. Write everything down in an uncritical, brain storming session. At the end of this session, in each quadrant, list all the agreed upon ideal scene goals.

Next, write down: CURRENT SCENE. This is simply where your community is now as it relates to where it has been articulated that you want to be. Begin then to create a draft of steps that will connect the dots between what is and what will be. Finally pray for a champion for each major endeavor. In the "Dream Kingdom Dreams," section, there is a draft of our New York City Ideal Scene. There is much to add and much to edit, but it is a starting point for building a John 17/Acts 1:8 city.

PREPARE FOR KINGDOM ENDURANCE

Prepare a strong infrastructure of committed leaders that will gear up for the long haul. A passion for unity does not mean, "Let's give it a shot for a few years." It can sometimes take decades to bring about healing in the fractured body of Christ. There will always be occasions when many will want to abandon the cause and return to isolated kingdom building. We must come to the point where we acknowledge that when classic American rugged individualism is adopted by the Church, it is heretical. Oneness must become our only option and a way of life.

There is so much at stake when cities come together in holy unity; we must all be prepared for vicious and violent spiritual warfare. Personally, while writing this book, it has been brutal and relentless.

PREPARE FOR EXPONENTIAL KINGDOM EXPANSION

It is the promise of God that when we are one with Him and each other, the world will know that Christ has been sent from the Father. Every step in this direction will lead to greater awakening. Therefore, we must prepare ourselves for the coming harvest. We must prepare our leadership and our disciples for overflow.

In addition at this point the coalition of churches can start to identify "church-forsaken" pockets in your city and neighboring cities and begin praying for church planting direction.

We believe that in the near future, our association will collectively reach out to an overseas city or nation.

DREAM KINGDOM DREAMS

"Write the vision; make it plain on tablets, so he may run who
reads it. For still the vision awaits its appointed time."
Habakkuk 2:3

The following is a simple strategic planning exercise which lays
out the NYC ideal scene for Saturation.

THE JERUSALEM COMMISSION

- We have a shepherd over every Borough in NYC and Long
  Island.
- We have a shepherd over all 59 Community Districts in
  NYC.
- Each CD shepherd has established a vibrant weekly pastoral
  prayer meeting in that CD.
- In that pastoral gathering are several churches representing
  every ZIP code in the CD.
- Each church has taken gospel responsibility for a clearly
  delineated portion of that ZIP code: their parish. The pur-
  pose is gospel/discipleship coverage. Not territorialism.
- Each church has teams that visit, pray for and evangelize
  every household in their parish.
- Each church is discipling the willing and caring for the desperate that they have encountered.
- Whenever a need is beyond the capacity of the parish church,
  they will report the situation to the larger coalition and seek
  to determine a collaborative solution.
- Parishes will and should overlap from time to time, as many

Gospel-centered churches are positioned in close proximity to one another. These churches should nurture and exemplify the highest level of unity and brotherly love, often praying together, assisting one another and planning outreaches together. Those who live within the borders of the parish should be encouraged to attend the Church they feel God has called them to and/or the one they feel most comfortable in.

- Every street and every apartment floor has a neighborhood shepherd who knows, prays for, and loves on their block or floor. Sometimes this will be a resident, other times an assigned prayer minister.

- The parish churches and neighborhood shepherds will know and love their community better than any other organization or institution in existence. Every home in a given parish will be visited on a regular basis, evangelized, loved, cared and prayed for. Every new believer will be discipled and nurtured in Christ.

THE JUDEA COMMISSION

- All the participating Churches in a given CD/region gather together quarterly to pray, hear from the Lord and strategize towards the goal of Gospel/Discipleship/Christian Compassion saturation in the entire city region. Deciding in community what they could do better together than separately.

- We have a team of contractors and blue collar believers who are tooled up and committed to helping our widows, orphans, seniors and disabled persons in distress.

- We have a fellowship of marketplace believers who pray together, and plan together for the purpose of Kingdom advancement in our city.

- They have created a "Christian Angie's List" to enable our business owners to flourish.
- They have created a suite of employment solutions for the floundering unemployed in our city.
- They have created a foundation that is being used for meaningful initiatives.
- They encourage one another and hold each other accountable for honorable living.

THE SAMARIA COMMISSION

- Every Housing Project or blighted community in the CD has been identified and is being consistently prayed for.
- Several churches, some local and others from more stable communities are involved in weekly visitation and regular outreach to each of these troubled communities.
- Partnerships with parachurch ministries (Metro World Child, Child Evangelism Fellowship, Young Life, and so on) are flourishing.
- Sports and other creative outreaches for teens, and ministry for children and young mothers is established.
- Parenting classes and marriage restoration classes are being offered along with mentoring.

THE ENDS OF THE EARTH COMMISSION

- The Church has empowered, enabled and equipped all of her members to evangelize, disciple and make disciplers of immigrants and internationals in NYC.
- The CD coalitions are reaching out beyond their borders to neighboring struggling communities

- The Borough coalitions are aligning their collective impact to adopt international cities and nations.
- In every CD, a careful analysis to identify pockets of immigrant groups has been done. Each unreached people group in NYC has been adopted in prayer and deed by one or several churches.

BATTLE KINGDOM FRUSTRATION

Let's be candid: most, if not all, evangelicals are frustrated revivalists. We often wonder why God doesn't "just do it." We implore, "Just let your glory fall, do what you did for Charles Finney and Jeremiah Lamphere." We have longed for an outpouring of power for so long and been so disappointed that we have stopped longing. It hurts to believe in revival.

John 17:22 gives us a different spin regarding the purposes of God's glory. Jesus said, "The glory which You have given Me, I have given to them, that they may be one, just as We are one." The purpose of God's glory come down is to give us power to "be one" with each other. The "weight of God's glory" is one of the most mysterious and awe-inspiring concepts in scripture. Christ received it and then gave it to the Church to empower us to be united. He is giving us the best that He has, power immeasurable, so that we can be miraculously and supernaturally close. It is the miracle of love that will open the floodgates of revival. Could it be that simple? The key to awakening is for families, churches, and the Church to love one another and work together.

I often need to renounce the subtle grumblings in my heart against God, the accusations of my spirit that He withholds His glory haphazardly, even callously. Jesus has already has given us His glory; we, however, have not utilized it for its intended purpose. Instead, when we experience a drop of God's glory, we make a show of it. When a great, outstanding miracle occurs in a city, it often becomes the impetus to showcase a ministry. All this produces the opposite effect: instead of engendering oneness, division, jealousy and glory-hoarding abound. Imagine God's sorrow when we use the precious treasure of His glory as a tool to market ourselves.

The Lord longs to pour out a blessing we cannot contain. He longs to gather us "together as a hen gathers her brood under her wings -- but we are too often, "not willing." (Matthew 23:37). Like Israel of old, we spurn His pleadings. The promise remains that revival will come when we are one.

If the Church in America obeyed Christ's appeal for our oneness and learned to serve together strategically, that alone would launch a worldwide revival. It has been calculated that if all the people of China jumped off a table at the same time, it would start a tsunami that would wipe out half of the United States. Imagine the holy flood the Church could launch! The sheer synergistic force of fifty million evangelicals loving one another and working together to build God's kingdom is unfathomable. What, then, on earth is wrong with us? Why is it so hard?

There are several explanations: a primary one being that Satan knows John 17 better than we do and devotes more energy than we could imagine to divide and conquer the Church. The Greek meaning of the word "devil" is "diabolos" or "one who throws between." Divider is his name. Day and night he works to divide us from God, the family of God and our loved ones. There is, however, a systemic lie, a spirit of the age that ever divides the Church yet does not require demonic intervention. Jesus detested it and we should as well. In

Chapter 4, we will ponder our Lord's zealous cleaning of the temple.

DISCUSSION QUESTIONS:

Note: Each of these questions correlates with one of the "Kingdom" sections listed within this chapter.

1. Kingdom Boundaries: What ministry districts and subdivisions of your region can you envision?

2. Kingdom Power: Write down three to five potential prayer partners.

3. Kingdom Potential: List down as many potential ministry partners as you can. Get creative: look at the list of churches and potential ministry partners and write down or discuss the possibilities.

4. Kingdom Synergy: Count the cost: Divide a sheet of paper in half. On one side, name the challenges of unity. On the other, number and name the potential outcomes of disunity.

5. Kingdom Saturation: Describe and/or discuss what you need to do to prepare for a prolonged noble battle. What hooks, entanglements or bitter roots are you aware of that need to be dealt with now, before you begin?

6. Kingdom Endurance: Confess any resentment you have harbored against God. Write down any divisive spirit that you struggle with. Renounce these sins, and pray for help in submitting to God and resisting the Devil.

CHAPTER FOUR

"I DID NOT COME TO MAKE BUSINESS"

A dear friend of mine spent many years serving in a Muslim nation in Central Asia. During his time on furlough, one of the young men that he had ministered to became a Christian. He excitedly shared his new found joy with his fiancé. She also became a Christian. She in turn spoke to one of her family members. News soon got to the young lady's parents. Immediately they broke off the engagement and married the young girl to an old Mullah. Soon after, the young lady committed suicide.

As my friend prepared to return to Asia, he did not know what would become of this young man after such tragedy. When they sat for tea, he asked, "Brother, how is your faith in Christ after all that has happened?" The young man responded with piercing simplicity and clarity: "When I came to Christ, I did not come to make business. I follow Christ because He is the truth."

"ZEAL FOR YOUR HOUSE CONSUMES ME"

Our Lord is called the Prince of Peace. He exemplified this throughout His entire ministry. When the angry mob was ready to throw him off a cliff, He walked right through them. When the Pharisees seemed to have Him trapped, He asked them a simple question and they were undone. When He was falsely accused and cruelly abused, He was like a lamb led to the slaughter. When they scourged him and nailed him to a tree, he said, "Father, forgive them for they know not what they do." But when he saw His Father's house made into a den of thieves…He righteously flipped out. One might say that He experienced the extremity of righteous indignation and holy anger.

We must pause and take note when God exhibits such extreme emotion.

> *The Passover of the Jews was near, and Jesus went up to Jerusalem. And He found in the temple those who were selling oxen and sheep and doves, and the money changers seated at their tables. And He made a scourge of cords, and drove them all out of the temple, with the sheep and the oxen; and He poured out the coins of the money changers and overturned their tables; and to those who were selling the doves He said, "Take these things away; stop making My Father's house a place of business." His disciples remembered that it was written, "ZEAL FOR YOUR HOUSE WILL CONSUME ME."*
>
> **John 2:13-17**

The focus of Christ's anger seems benign at first glance: "Stop making my father's house a place of business." Maybe "stop making my Father's house a place of harlotry or witchcraft" would merit such a violent response, but was all that mayhem really about "business?" Is a business mindset in the church really such a bad thing?

Isn't there much to be learned from the corporate giants that dominate our nation? We'd all like to go from "Good to Great." We all could use more efficiency and excellence. Obviously jettisoning all corporate wisdom is not reasonable and flies against our Biblical admonition that all things be done "decently and in order" (I

Corinthians 14:40).

What then enraged our gentle Savior? Fans of the Godfather trilogy might recall the underlying rationale that was consistently employed to justify betrayal, extortion and murder: "It's not personal…strictly business."

We would be hard-pressed to find a nation as addicted and devoted to materialism as the USA. It is the "spirit of the age;" the zeitgeist in the air that Americans breathe. There have always been kings and emperors who were obsessed with gold, but we live in a nation that preaches, exalts, idolizes and moralizes greed. From the richest to the poorest, from Wall Street to Church Street, from the cradle to the grave, the creed "Greed is good" dominates our culture.

I am not prepared to argue the virtue of economic and political systems. My grave concern is that the Church has lost its bearings within the vast American ocean of commercialism and materialism. This love of success and money has seduced the Church and made it her mistress.

> There have always been kings and emperors who were obsessed with gold, but we live in a nation that preaches, exalts, idolizes and moralizes greed.

The business/marketplace value system that we have fully embraced has set us on a course towards certain destruction. There are far too many churches and ministries today that operate primarily by the "bottom line" principle. Too many board meetings have pivoted on this sentiment: "Don't give me all that spiritual stuff, what's the bottom line? Is it financially sustainable? What is the ROI (return on investment)…etc."

This mindset can kill Godly vision and radical faith-filled initiatives before they get off the ground. This is not to condone foolishness. But woe to us if we forget that the only important bottom line is this: "What is the heart of God in this matter?" No matter how we rationalize the need for fiscal wisdom and responsibility, the love of profit is still the root of all kinds of evil (I Timothy 6:10).

Zero to negative Church growth is inexplicable in the United States. We have spent billions of dollars on outreach, advertising and marketing our faith. We have recorded awe-inspiring, cutting-edge worship music, trained captivating preachers, and produced incredible films and videos. We have even grown churches that fill stadiums; yet still we find ourselves in a state of dangerous decline.

Great stories of "revival" are, upon closer examination, rarely anything more than transfer growth. It's similar to when Walmart opens up a new location and experiences tremendous success – by putting several mom and pop stores out of business.

Clearly our decline in attendance, morality, passion and cultural impact reveal a Church of our own fashioning, not His. I'm sure there are many factors, but I venture to say that the spirit of the age, the capitalist mindset, the competitive business model and corporate church mentality has done incalculable damage to the body of Christ. There are a multitude of tentacles that spring from this unholy marriage of the Church and Mammon; we will explore a few.

COMPETITORS VS. CO-LABORERS

There is nothing on the earth more powerful than the light of the sun. Yet we, the saints, are the divinely empowered lights of the world. There is no political scheme, no atheistic agenda and no diabolical conspiracy that could ever stop us. We are only stopped when we turn our power against one another. When we adopt a business model, there is no escaping the dark reality that we are in competition with one another. If we continue to operate in this fashion, failure is our only option. The words of Christ are piercing: "Every kingdom divided against itself is laid waste, and a divided household falls" (Luke 11:17).

On D-Day, the Allied Forces launched one of the most collaborative international military operations in the history of modern warfare. Ground troops, naval forces, air and commando units from America, Great Britain, France, Canada, Poland and Norway all synchronized, synergized and strategized to break the back of the Axis powers and Hitler's Germany.

The Battle of Normandy was one of the costliest, most complex and most important battles of the 20th Century. Organizing and orchestrating the Allied Forces was among the most daunting tasks of WWII. Nevertheless, victory was impossible apart from it.

The Church of Jesus Christ is embroiled in a similar battle of epic proportions. These are challenging days. We must come together or perish. We understand these truths in the natural realm. If the Allied forces fought amongst themselves, if they failed to coordinate or communicate, we would all be speaking German right now. If our own Navy, Army, Air Force and Marines did the same today, our nation would be doomed.

In a business-driven church culture, the sweet saints can turn bitter. Friendly church competition can get ugly when one party is losing. It can devolve into war overnight. We have all seen church leaders undermine and trash-talk a neighboring church. As a young Christian I learned that clear battle lines were drawn by pastors. Flocks were retained by bad mouthing the surrounding churches theology, morality, biblical loyalty, or even the car the pastor drove. One church constantly demonized any other church that didn't use the King James Bible. I was verbally assaulted by one of my members who had been swayed by this toxic and divisive teaching.

This spirit of competition corrupts even the holy things: "Who has the best worship team, best prayer ministry, who is the best preacher?" These questions are too often the driving force in congregants choosing or leaving a church. Jealously and resentment will always poison competing ministries. The longer this mindset is tolerated, the more fractured the church and its surrounding community will become. We are the blood-bought, mercy-drenched children of God. If we can't get along and lead in love, no one will get along.

I was privileged to observe an amazing antithesis to the "pastor/competitor" model during and after Hurricane Sandy. One of the leading pastors in our coalition, Rev. John Carlo, current vice president of the Staten Island Association of Evangelicals, reacted heroically in a multitude of ways. Our first gathering after the storm was held at his church (Christian Pentecostal Church) and it remained the command center and "Hub Church" for almost a year.

> We are the blood-bought, mercy-drenched children of God. If we can't get along and lead in love, no one will get along.

During the months of relief and recovery, CPC worked very closely with Rev. Steve Martino of Movement Church. Steve powerfully spearheaded the "parish" outreach in the particularly hard hit region of New Dorp Beach. Not only did he rebuild dozens of damaged homes, his work was so effective that he received a grant from Joyce Meyers Ministry to rebuild a storefront and plant a church in the area that he served.

For over a year, CPC continued to support Pastor Steve's outreach and help him build his new church. By this time the overwhelming crisis of the storm had passed and most of the churches were attempting to return to a semblance of normalcy. Nevertheless, CPC's executive pastor, Rev. Joseph Chevere, who had construction experience, worked side by side with Pastor Steve from start to finish.

Another Pastor in our association, Chris Dito, installed the floor. Several other churches gave funds to help Steve complete his facility in time for a heavenly opening service. CPC received no earthly gain from their service, but the eternal rewards and bonds of love are priceless.

CONSUMERS VS. CONGREGANTS

If pastors look at one another as competitors instead of brothers and fellow soldiers on the same mission, passion for the lost is often replaced with small-minded territorialism. Servanthood is then trumped by selfish ambition and often the abuse of authority.

In the worst of cases, instead of servant leadership, "sheep" are manipulated for gain. They become pawns in a sick game where ministries compete for tithes, crowds and servants to serve the man and the machine. Pastors with this mindset end up competing like billionaires to see their names emblazoned in the Christian Fortune 500 Club. The lost sheep that Jesus wept over are viewed as trophies in a numbers game or as "another tithing family."

In better (or somewhat healthier) business scenarios; congregations are treated like customers, and Churches in turn are treated like retail stores. Whoever offers the best bargains, the best service and the best atmosphere wins the day. Even when a ministry thrives using this paradigm, the consumer-driven Church is a double-edged sword.

Often, well-intentioned Pastors unwittingly adopt a business model for their church to their own demise. The darkest day in a pastor's life is the one in which he realizes that many of those that he has prayed with, cried with, baptized and discipled consider him to be half friend, and half commodity. The "Church as business" model trains our people to shop for the best deal in town. How can we concurrently expect the local church loyalty that we long for?

> The darkest day in a pastor's life is the one in which he realizes that many of those that he has prayed with, cried with, baptized and discipled consider him to be half friend, half commodity.

We have all seen congregants "hop" from church to church in a city, instigating bitterness, jealously, backbiting, even hatred between local Pastors and congregations. This commonly accepted lifestyle serves to divide the Church. These painful wounds will often be the main reason why church leaders will not pray together.

BRANDING VS. SOLIDARITY

In his recent book, *Stand Out*, Marcus Buckingham writes: "How can you elevate your performance and become a lynchpin, the proverbial franchise player, the one whom they tell stories about at company gatherings, the one whom the biggest and best clients request?[1]" This book is suggested reading for pastors! This may be par for the course in the corporate world, but it is disastrous in the Church. How does this mindset align with "He must increase, but I must decrease?" (John 3:30)

How does this mindset align with our foot-washing Savior, "Who, though he was in the form of God, did not count equality with

1. Marcus Buckingham. *Stand Out* (Nashville, TN: Thomas Nelson, 2011).

God a thing to be grasped, but emptied himself, by taking the form of a servant, being born in the likeness of men. And being found in human form, he humbled himself by becoming obedient to the point of death, even death on a cross." (Philippians 2:5-8) Paul goes on to explain that God highly exalted Him. Jesus did not exalt himself.

Standing out or "branding," is a standard, universally accepted and expected business practice. If a business wants to thrive, they must do so by distinguishing and distancing their commodity or company from their competition. All marketing is centered on elevating a particular brand above the fray. The question is, should this marketing norm be adopted by the local church? "You've tried the rest, now try the best" is fine if you are opening a pizzeria, but it is a divisive and disastrous practice when applied to the local church. This is not to say that we should neglect to present ourselves well in our cities and communities. It would be wise, however, to frame every marketing decision as a large conglomerate (ie. GE or Johnson and Johnson) might. The leadership of a large multisite, multi-faceted company would advertise in such a way so as to benefit all those under their vast umbrella. If partnering churches in given communities embraced a similar marketing strategy, in the long run, it would benefit both the local church and the regional Church.

One example of this that is in its infancy is our collective website, www.newlife4SI. New Life 4SI is how we are "branding" and marketing our association of churches. All of our partnering ministries are represented on this website. Whenever someone logs on to look for a church, the website points them to several churches in their vicinity. They are given the opportunity to peruse the web pages of several churches to find a place that suits them. All of our collaborative outreaches and much of our individual outreach material include this link so that seekers who attend large events can find a church that is close to them and "clicks" for them.

Always pitching for the regional church can, however, be challenging when it comes to growing our own ministries and meeting our financial needs. In my personal context, the church I pastor and the non-profit that we began, Urban Hope NYC, have been working for months on a very ambitious outreach aimed at reaching the most at-risk population in our blighted communities: young men between 13 and 20 years old. This winter we are planning to launch a basketball league that will reach around 500 of these disconnected youth in Staten Island's Housing Projects. I would have loved to call this league the "Urban Hope Basketball League." We are experiencing strong support and buy in from both community and marketplace leaders. The league is our dream child. It would be very good business for us to banner and promote Urban Hope through it. Good business for us, bad for the kingdom of God, bad for the thousands of disconnected youth in our borough and bad for the collective impact of the Church of Staten Island. The name of the league is instead, "New Life4SI Basketball League." We have chaplains and several partnering churches in place who will be ministering to these young people in the four most challenging communities of our borough. The true kingdom impact of this league would be greatly decreased if we sought after a marketing opportunity. We are not here to "make business." It is our God who will supply our needs "according to His riches in glory." (Phil. 4:19)

In a recent gathering of NYC ministry leaders, Rev. Robert Guerrero spoke from the Beatitudes. In particular he shared some thoughts about the nature of salt. That "salt is most effective when it is invisible. It is most offensive, however, when it is highly visible." These are the musings of the people of God, and this is the heartbeat of our Savior. His revolutionary declaration was that the greatest among us would be the servant of all.

INBREEDING VS. BALANCE AND ACCOUNTABILITY

The inescapable fruit of a "free-market capitalism" approach to church growth is polarization and isolation. Branding necessitates highlighting what is unique, different and better about your product. It breeds a hunger to be the innovator with the new ice cream flavor or "special sauce" that brings in the crowds. In church circles, it may sound more like, "come and experience the new anointing," or "come to hear truly biblically based preaching." Most of the time, this approach distances ministries from one another. It's hard to pray with someone and serve your city together when you are trying to prove to your region that your brand is superior to theirs. Distancing your company from the competition is essential. Pastors from competing churches will rarely be friends. Isolation of this sort will always lead to inbreeding.

Social inbreeding replicates and exacerbates genetic defects in an incestuous community. Inbreeding in Christian communities can easily lead to imbalance and heresy. We have all seen different movements become extreme and sometimes toxic when they are isolated and inbred. God designed our reproductive system to screen out genetic defects in normal social systems. Similarly, having meaningful relationship with Christian leaders who honor the word of God but hold to different theological distinctions, engenders healthy dialogue and eventually, more balanced doctrine. When communication is shut down and ministry leaders are labeled and/or demonized by one another, there is no accountability, no loving, robust debate and no iron sharpening iron. On the contrary, cohorts of ministers and followers who think and feel the same way gather in protected silos that often incubate heresy.

I had many pre-conceived notions about some pastors on Staten Island. These notions were borne out of gossip, passing anecdotes, and in some cases, just a bad "vibe." After reaching out and meeting with them, I was embarrassed when I realized how quickly I had dismissed and unfairly labeled them. Today, they are some of my best friends. Many of us came from different denominational and theological streams. It has been interesting to observe that over the years, as the result of healthy conversation and friendship, we all seem to be moving towards a more biblically based theological sweet spot.

The word of God warns us that "we see in a mirror dimly...we know in part and we prophesy in part (I Cor. 9,13). None of us have the corner on theology or practice. None of us fully understand the mystery of prayer, the workings of the Holy Spirit or the Sovereignty of God. It is very important to engage in prayer and humble dialogue with those who serve in our cities and communities. In Ephesians 4:13, we are admonished to walk in this manner, "until we all attain to the unity of the faith and the knowledge of the Son of God, to mature manhood, to the measure of the stature of the fullness of Christ." The full context of this verse punctuates the necessity of this kind of rich and holy fellowship.

And he gave the apostles, the prophets, the evangelists, the shepherds, and teachers, to equip the saints for the work of ministry, for building up the body of Christ, until we all attain to the unity of the faith and of the knowledge of the Son of God, to mature manhood, to the measure of the stature of the fullness of Christ, so that we may no longer be children, tossed to and fro by the waves and carried about by every wind of doctrine, by human cunning, by craftiness in deceitful schemes. Rather, speaking the truth in love, we are to grow up in every way into him who is the head, into Christ, from whom the whole body, joined and held together by every joint with which it is equipped, when each part is working properly, makes the body grow so that it builds itself up in love.

Ephesians 4:11-16

HIRED HANDS VS. SHEPHERDS AFTER GOD'S HEART

I recently spoke at a gathering of pastors in eastern Pennsylvania about the concept of reaching our "Samarias," our blighted and devastated neighborhoods and communities. A minister from Kenya approached me during the lunch break.

He said, "I want you to bring this message to Kenya. There are thousands of refugees streaming into our country because of the wars and unrest that surround our nation, but the Church does nothing to help these people. It is because they will bring no financial gain to the church that they are ignored. We have been poisoned with the prosperity Gospel and it is destroying us."

Unfortunately, this sentiment is not confined to Kenya. The best opportunity for financial gain is to draw a tithing church member from another church. Whether this is done intentionally or passively, the results are the same. When churches target the "already saved," the lost and the poor become lower and lower in priority.

After pastoring an inner-city church for over 20 years, we have learned that it is God who sustains His house; not six figure tithing families. Our neighborhood families struggle greatly. In the past year we have helped to rescue four of our families from eviction.

We do not charge a penny for any of our 11-month community children's outreach. If we did, the children who needed the ministry most would be excluded. We understand this is mission, not business. We don't expect big money to come in from our neighborhoods. We do expect the Lord to take care of us as we dedicate ourselves to take care of the poor.

It has been a very long and challenging road, but the Lord has sustained us; paid off our mortgage, rebuilt our church, covered the salaries of four staff members and recently gifted and installed a commercial kitchen for us. We have lived on "manna" for over twenty years. It is not pleasant at times, but God has supplied all of our needs every step of the way.

Isaiah 58:10-11 offers a counter-cultural perspective on fiscal sustainability:

If you pour yourself out for the hungry and satisfy the desire of the afflicted, then shall your light rise in the darkness, and your gloom be as the noonday. And the Lord will guide you continually and satisfy your desire in scorched places, and make your bones strong; and you shall be like a watered garden, like a spring of water, whose waters do not fail.

A church without compassion for the alien, the oppressed and the widow and orphan in distress is frighteningly far from the mark. The words of Christ from the Sermon on the Mount are piercing:

If then the light in you is darkness, how great is the darkness! No one can serve two masters, for either he will hate the one and love the other, or he will be devoted to the one and despise the other. You cannot serve God and money.

Matthew 6:23, 24

There is a tender vignette that is often unnoticed amidst the shock and awe of the Temple cleansing. It reveals another reason for God's righteous indignation. It was after Jesus cleared the Temple of the money changers that: "...the blind and the lame came to him in the temple, and he healed them" (Matthew 21:14).

When the Lord's house is a place of business, the "least of these" are trampled underfoot. We must root out this mindset and retire it permanently. We must track down and retrieve the many spores of wickedness it has birthed. We cannot go on building our own house and neglecting the House of the Lord (Haggai 1:7-10). Jesus promised that "the gates of hell shall not prevail" against the Church that He builds (Matthew 16:18). Is He building His Church through us, or are we building a tower of Babel for our own name sake?" The current inefficacy of the Church in America tragically indicates the latter.

THE STATURE OF THE FULLNESS OF CHRIST

Throughout his epistles, Paul casts a vision for one Church, one Temple and one body, "one Lord, one faith, one baptism, one God and Father of all, who is over all and through all and in all. (Eph. 4:5,6). Sadly, this vision is hard to swallow. We often sub-consciously dismiss the obvious will of God because it has become foreign to us. We must be cognizant of our bend towards division. Over the centuries, the Church has devolved into a haphazard, schismatic and fiercely independent movement. We have splintered and fractured to such an extreme degree that we find it hard to fathom functional unity.

Nevertheless, even in our splintered state, there is no other force for good worthy of comparison. Those that have managed to thrive can be likened to powerful feudal lords who, despite the lack of a unified military force, protected their towns and cities against all odds. They have overcome and kept the faith because the love of Christ compels them, and the fire of His Spirit burns within. I firmly believe that these overcomers long to correct the divisive trajectory of their forefathers.

Many saints and leaders continue to share a unified love for God, His Word and the Great Commission. These three points of agreement can be considered the cords of oneness that have enabled God's people to consistently be salt and light. There are millions of noble lords who are ready and willing to lay down their own banners and raise only the banner of Christ. They wait patiently for the battle plan, for a unifying structure. They long to dwell in, build up and expand outward the House of the Lord. I believe that God is birthing a revival centered on John 17; one that will inspire and enable coordinated and synergistic ministry throughout the earth.

DISCUSSION QUESTIONS:

1. What have you done, or what would you like to do, to keep a Godly mindset in a marketplace driven culture?

2. What practical steps can you take to ensure that the Lord's house is a "house of prayer" instead of a den of robbers?

3. Which of the business models discussed do you find yourself most embroiled in? What steps can you take to reset or reboot your ministry?

4. On a scale of 1 to 10 (with 10 being the most independent), would you rate yourself as fiercely independent lone ranger or desperately interdependent? What has contributed to this attitude?

CHAPTER FIVE
A TALE OF THREE TEMPLES

This book began with a burden for my "Samaria." The subject matter is very personal to me because I love the children and families in the troubled neighborhood that I serve. In all honesty, I don't see real hope for change in my community and thousands more like it if the Church clings to its feudalistic status quo.

While writing this chapter, I was on the phone with pastor friends, police, and congregants because of two young men that attended our "Yogi Bear" children's outreach ten years ago. One killed the other across the street from my church. The perpetrator was hiding somewhere and I had to locate his family, as the relatives of the murdered young man were talking about vengeance.

Both young men were seventeen years old. The murder took place in the home of one of the sweetest seven-year-olds in our after-school program. She was in her bedroom with her little sister when John* was shot four times by a "friend." As you read this, please pray for her; a blood-splattered teenager's body, terror, and screams of anguish are etched into her psyche forever.

Another junior high school girl that has been in many of our after-school and summer camp programs is the little sister of the murderer. She was rescued at her junior high school from knife-wielding eighth graders sent to cut or kill her. This girl received numerous death threats on Facebook. Her entire family was terrified.

The depth of brokenness and sorrow in these two families alone is unbearable. Yet there are a million people in the housing projects of my city coping with the weight of similar tragedy and fear.

We do everything we can to help the families and children of our neighborhood rise above the dangers that surround them, but it's complicated. The challenges, immense as they are, are not simple equations to solve. Our church alone is not able to meet the vast need.

I do believe, however, that the whole Church, with "the fullness of Him who fills everything in every way" (Ephesians 1:23, NIV) is more than enough.

As we seek to fulfill our charge to strategically and collaboratively reach out to our Jerusalem, Judea, Samaria and the ends of the earth, we believe that we are fulfilling an important aspect of our New Covenant Temple directive. Many of us now dream of the day when every household, in every ZIP code, has a neighborhood shepherd from a local church. We dream of the day when each NYC public school and housing project is prayed for and cared for by local churches. We dream that coalitions of churches will adopt city after city nationally and internationally.

As we (the old men) dream dreams, and the next generation sees visions, there is a sense of completion, a sense that we are fulfilling our purposes for our generation (Acts 13:36). We feel the favor of God as we savor these dreams in our hearts. We feel the witness of the Spirit that we are on the right path to finishing our New Covenant Temple Commission.

Throughout this work, we have been pondering the parallels between our Great Commission and the three Great Temple Commissions of the Moses, Solomon and Jesus. A closer examination of this comparison can help our discussion.

IS IT FINISHED?

Redemptive history can be described as "a tale of three temples." The completed work can be framed as the grand finale to an epic orchestral piece, the glorious crowning chapter of a story woven throughout the centuries. Each completion of the Lord's house was one of God's pinnacle moments. I think of them as His sweetest earthly memories. Each was the next step to the restoration of the intimacy and oneness that He shared in Eden with His beloved children.

Many of us have had similar pinnacle moments: broken marriages healed and made new, prodigals restored. As we ponder our moments of inexpressible joy, we are given a window into the joy of the Father's heart when His beloved ones come home. As we set our hearts to be twenty-first century temple builders, we set them to bring joy to God and the world.

> As we ponder our moments of inexpressible joy, we are given a window into the joy of the Father's heart when His beloved ones come home.

You see, for God, the tale of three temples is a very personal tale. His children are lost and homeless, and He sends out his Church to find them and bring them home. When the Church is fractured, the Lord's house is structurally compromised and unappealing. When we continually circumvent our "Samarias," the least of these are forgotten. When we neglect our "Jerusalem", the neighbors and co-workers that God has placed next to us remain sheep without a Shepherd. When we disregard the "ends of the earth," God's heart grieves for those in distant lands that haven't heard the good news.

Completing the building of the Temple means far more to God than we can comprehend. With each ancient Temple completion, glory falls, as if God cannot contain his joy. In each Temple scenario, we see repeated a clear pattern of work finished and glory filling the House.

1.   Moses completed the Tabernacle, he finished his Great Commission and glory filled the House.

> *He erected the court all around the tabernacle and the altar, and hung up the veil for the gateway of the court. Thus Moses finished the work. Then the cloud covered the tent of meeting, and the glory of the Lord filled the tabernacle.*
> **Exodus 40:33-34**

2.   Solomon completed the Temple, he finished his Great Commission and glory filled the House.

> *Thus all the work that Solomon did for the house of the Lord was finished... When the priests came out of the Holy Place and all the Levitical singers... they praised the Lord saying, "He indeed is good for His loving kindness is everlasting;" then the house, the house of the Lord, was filled with a cloud, and the glory of the Lord filled the house of God.*
> **2 Chronicles 5: 1-14**

3.   Jesus cried out "it is finished," our souls were redeemed, and glory filled the Church.

> *Jesus, knowing that all things had already been accomplished to fulfill the Scripture, said, "It is finished."*
> **John 19:28, 30.**

The parallel is clear. Jesus satisfied every detailed requirement, fulfilled every messianic prophecy, bore every sorrow, and paid for every sin. Now "the House of the Lord" is built inside the heart of everyone who will call upon His name to be saved. The saints can be sanctified and given the privilege of becoming living, breathing, Temples of God!

Our Carpenter King built a new kind of house with his nail-pierced hands. The Apostle Paul conclusively declared, "Don't you know that you yourselves are God's temple and that God's Spirit lives in you?" (I Corinthians 3:16).

On Pentecost Sunday, a new kind of glory filled the Lord's house:

When the day of Pentecost arrived, they were all together in one place. And suddenly there came from heaven a sound like a mighty rushing wind, and it filled the entire house where they were sitting. And divided tongues as of fire appeared to them and rested on each one of them. And they were all filled with the Holy Spirit and began to speak in other tongues as the Spirit gave them utterance.

Acts 2:1-4

4. There is a temptation to see Pentecost as the final crowning jewel, the last chapter of the epic "Tale of Three Temples." It would be wiser to see this wondrous day as the glorious "Grand Opening Celebration of the New Covenant Temple." The proactive, intentional expansion of the living Temple of Christ still remains our greatest commission. The saints from the upper room understood this and immediately filled Jerusalem with the great news and the blessing of the Holy Spirit. Soon they and their converts would be scattered throughout Judea, Samaria and the ends of the earth (Acts 8).

My dear Church History professor, Dr. Harold Shelly, shared

with me his wonder at seeing a statue of Andrew the Apostle in the Ukraine. Tradition tells us that St. Andrew reached and preached the Gospel at the Black Sea, nearly a thousand miles from Jerusalem. These saints and apostles obeyed well the full charge of their Great Commission. They traveled and traversed the known world with their "beautiful feet" (Romans 10:15; Isaiah 52:7). The pattern continues to play out as the Apostles "finish" their first assignments. After Pentecost in Jerusalem, we read of God's glory falling in Samaria, then upon a Roman Centurion and all his household (Judea), finally upon an Ethiopian Eunuch (to the Ends of the Earth)

> *The church throughout all Judea and Galilee and Samaria had*
> *peace and was being built up. Walking in the fear of the Lord and*
> *in the comfort of the Holy Spirit, it multiplied.*
> **Acts 9:31**

Here we see a different expression of completion. Obviously the entirety of the work was not and is not finished, but the trajectory of the mission was set in motion. They followed the instructions given in Acts 1:8.

The entire book of Acts is the story of glory falling everywhere the apostles put their feet. The exciting visual is that of the Temple of God springing forth in Jerusalem, Judea, Samaria and in every tribe, tongue and nation. In Acts 2, we see everyone from every nation being baptized in the Holy Spirit. In Acts 8, 9 and 10, we see new believers actively reaching out to their region, to Samaria and even to the Gentiles. Specifically in Acts 8:17, we see a kind of "Samaritan Pentecost," and in Acts 10:44, a "Gentile Pentecost." Soon the Apostle Paul and many others would bring the Gospel to the ends of the earth.

The short news flash quoted above in Acts 9:31 relays the joy of a fully-functioning, rightly-focused Church: "being built up...walking in the fear of the Lord...in the comfort of the Holy Spirit and multiplying." Already, the Gospel was being preached and people were being baptized in water and fire. Already, they were making disciples in all four quadrants of the Great Commission.

This new Temple of flesh and blood could not be contained in any house or city. The "Christ in Us" Temple is designed and empowered to encompass the earth. It is through Christ in us that streams of living water flow, ever filling the earth with His glory. We, His Kingdom of Priests and living stones, are the glory-bearers and Temple-builders.

New Testament scholar G.K. Beale, in his amazing theological treatise, *The Temple and the Church's Mission*, writes:

> *The new creation and Jerusalem are none other than God's tabernacle, the true temple of God's special presence...It was this divine presence that was formerly limited to Israel's Temple... [that] began to expand through the church, and which will fill the whole earth and heaven, becoming co-equal with it. Then the eschatological goal of the temple of the Garden of Eden dominating the entire creation will be finally fulfilled.* [1]

The people of God have always been a kingdom of priests and temple builders. The call to build the House of the Lord dominates the biblical landscape. Haggai's piercing words are as relevant to the 21st Century Church as they were when they were first penned.

---

1 G.K Beale. *The Temple and the Church's Mission.* (Downe's Grove, Illinois: IVP Academic, 2004), 368.

Then the word of the LORD came by the hand of Haggai the prophet, "Is it a time for you yourselves to dwell in your paneled houses, while this house lies in ruins? Now, therefore, thus says the LORD of hosts: Consider your ways. You have sown much, and harvested little. You eat, but you never have enough; you drink, but you never have your fill. You clothe yourselves, but no one is warm. And he who earns wages does so to put them into a bag with holes. Thus says the LORD of hosts: Consider your ways. Go up to the hills and bring wood and build the house, that I may take pleasure in it and that I may be glorified, says the Lord. You looked for much, and behold, it came to little. And when you brought it home, I blew it away. Why? declares the LORD of hosts. Because of my house that lies in ruins, while each of you busies himself with his own house. Therefore the heavens above you have withheld the dew, and the earth has withheld its produce. And I have called for a drought on the land and the hills, on the grain, the new wine, the oil, on what the ground brings forth, on man and beast, and on all their labors."
Haggai 1:3-11

Sadly, the only time this scripture is expounded upon in our contemporary evangelical setting seems to be during a church-building campaign. But God's House is not our local church. God's house is designed to accomplish much bigger things. We are His Great Commission contractors. The basic structural components that we have been addressing of "blueprint (Acts 1:8) and glue (John 17)," are foundational to the expansion and advance of God's kingdom.

Our Temple is designed and intended to fill the earth. This requires the kind of geographic and cultural directives we see embedded in Acts 1:8. The simplicity of this four-quadrant plan enables coalitions of Churches to strategically saturate every square inch and every cultural sector of their region. The "ends of the earth" challenge calls for constant expansion and replication.

Neglecting any portion of this quadrilateral plan is comparable to Moses completing half or three-quarters of the Tabernacle. It would be unfinished and without glory. In the context of the New Covenant Temple, our unfinished business, tragically, results in the neglect of God's lambs, His children. Whether it is our neighbors, the least of these, the outcasts, or those in far off lands, we have a compelling and comprehensive great commission to fulfill. Failure or neglect is not an option.

> Neglecting any portion of this quadrilateral plan is comparable to Moses completing half or three-quarters of the Tabernacle. It would be unfinished and without glory.

When then will we be able to say of our twenty-first century Temple, "It is finished?" Will glory be withheld until the entire Church is operating in oneness and synchronicity? Of course not. Again, the key is trajectory. There was never a time when the Levites were perfectly obedient. Moses didn't construct a perfect, flawless Tabernacle. Even the tabernacle, although faithfully constructed according to God's plan, was still a tent in the desert. Yet it was Moses' full-hearted attempt to honor God's instructions that opened the "ancient doors" (Psalm 24:7).

None of our attempts at unity will be perfected until we reach heaven. Yet we have all experienced the ever-increasing glory that follows a noble or godly trajectory. We have felt the blessing of His glory at a personal level when we are no longer double-minded, but fully given over to Christ. We know the glory that comes when family dwells together in unity, "like the precious oil on the head, running down…on the beard of Aaron" (Psalm 133:2).

We have beheld glory in our local church when hearts beat and burn as one. Many of us have even experienced the sweet grace of many congregations worshipping and working together in concert. With each expanding concentric circle, we experience increasing glory. We may not see its fullness in our lifetime, but we can set the trajectory in every city for ever-increasing glory.

As we think of all the players in the tale of three temples, it is humbling. Prophets, kings, priests, peasants and warriors have all been intricate parts of this great plan to restore heaven to earth. We are the players in the finale of finales. We are the Church, the "Ecclesia," the gathering. The baton has been handed to us to finish our Temple commission.

We have much to learn from King David's passion for the Lord's House. He set the stage for the next generation. Out of all of God's choice servants, only David was called, "a man after God's own heart."

> *And when he had removed him, he raised up David to be their*
> *king, of whom he testified and said, 'I have found in David the*
> *son of Jesse a man after my heart, who will do all my will.'*
> **Acts 13:22**

There seems to be a symbiotic relationship between a heart for God and a heart for His house. Very few have honored the "Shema" as holistically as King David. He poured his heart, soul, mind, strength and treasure into setting everything in place so that His son Solomon, might build a "house of rest for the ark of the covenant" (1 Chron. 28:2). Let us as well pour out our heart, soul, mind and strength to worship the King of glory and build His holy house. With every holy endeavor to come together and build up the New Covenant Temple, earth becomes more like heaven.

Remember, O Lord, in David's favor,
all the hardships he endured,
how he swore to the Lord
and vowed to the Mighty One of Jacob,
"I will not enter my house
or get into my bed,
I will not give sleep to my eyes
or slumber to my eyelids,
until I find a place for the Lord,
a dwelling place for the Mighty One of Jacob.

Psalm 132: 1-5

DISCUSSION QUESTIONS:

1.. Write down one facet from each of the three "Temple Stories" that capture your imagination.

2. Write down several facets from some of the Temple rebuilding and restoring stories that you feel are relevant to your spiritual journey and the journey of your community.

3. Earlier in this document you were asked to create an ideal scene for your city. Let's take it a step further. Take some time now to dream about what your city or community would look like if it were "on _____ (insert the name of our area) as it is in heaven." Dream about Eden restored, the Temple of God flourishing on all sides and in all ways. Describe your vision. Pray, believe and plan for it.

How strange it is that even in our modern era, so often mankind's greatest threat is infinitesimal? Cancer, Ebola, AIDS: these are some of the most terrifying words in the English language. Mysterious, imperceptible, microscopic invaders and dysfunctional cells attack the invisible building blocks of our bodies, bringing havoc, pain, and death. Their attacks hijack and confuse their hosts at the cellular level, distorting the cells' functionality and often triggering deadly accelerated growth and reproduction.

The Body of Christ, national and international, is only as strong as the living cells and living stones that are being replicated. The focus of this work is to present a macro-view of the Church. Yet it would be incomplete without addressing the impact of the building blocks of the larger edifice. We must consistently ask ourselves, "How is my church functioning at the cellular level?"

Our personal health can be quickly assessed by taking a blood sample and closely examining a few cells. What would a "blood sample" examination of the body of Christ in America reveal? Is there personal integrity and true worship in the hearts of the individual saints? Is there love and cohesion in our families? Is there healthy outreach and neighborly love being demonstrated? Is there allegiance to one Body and purpose?

We must ask the harder question as well: "Are our churches cancerous?"

Thousands of men and women have died prematurely because

they were afraid to properly and regularly check for cancer. Early detection is often life-saving. Cancer can spread quietly for many years. Ironically, it is often a disease related to over-production. High numerical growth is not always a sign of health. If we are rapidly reproducing unhealthy saints, that is definitively cancer. Just as cancer attacks the young and the old, the healthy and the weak, large and small churches alike must regularly assess the health of their people.

A large church could be artificially pumped up with hypocrisy, hype, and heresy. A small church could be ingrown, self-absorbed, and atrophied. Conversely, many large churches inspire thousands of passionate saints to reach the nations for Christ. Many small churches are like commando units assigned to unique and challenging battlefronts. In either case, the diagnostic key is the cell, the building block, the disciple, the living stone.

> Large and small churches alike must regularly assess the spiritual health of their people.

Without healthy cells that reproduce more healthy cells, or vibrant living stones that reproduce more living stones, there is no point in dreaming about reaching cities, fulfilling the Great Commission or building the New Covenant Temple.

It is fascinating to see that the great Acts 1:8 strategic plan is launched with individual tongues of fire falling on the disciples gathered in the upper room. He promised, "You will receive power when the Holy Spirit has fallen upon you and you will be my witnesses." No matter how vast and comprehensive the campaign, no one is exempt from the daily need to be saturated with and filled with the Holy Spirit. There can be no Kingdom Saturation without Personal Saturation. Whatever our theological leanings may be, there is no true saint that I have ever known who is not desperate for more of God's Holy Spirit.

It is Christ's Spirit in us that compels us to love our brother and sister in Christ so as to walk in oneness of purpose. It is Christ in us that compels us to reach out to the lost and broken. We must "build and be" a house of worship and a sanctuary of rescue.

When I found an old abandoned warehouse across the street from the West Brighton housing projects, I felt that it would be the perfect place for a community church. However, there was another church less than a block away from the warehouse that had been there for more than fifty years.

Before I made any plans to purchase the warehouse, I approached the pastor of this church. I told him I was considering planting a church there, but would not even consider it if he felt that I was trying to horn in on his territory. His reply makes me chuckle to this day: "Brother, there's plenty sinners in West Brighton."

Brothers and sisters: "There's plenty sinners everywhere."

As we consider Christ's hunger for the many sheep without a shepherd in our cities and communities, we must take a fresh look at discipleship within the context of the New Covenant Temple. It is far beyond the scope of this book to address "the making of a solid disciple." My desire in this chapter is merely to stir a broader "inter-church" view of regional ministry. There are very few churches that are capable of being "all-inclusive ministries." A practice of thinking outside the box of our local church would be transformational.

As I mentioned earlier, if Moses prepared and commissioned the Levites without simultaneously building the Tabernacle, all the training in the world would have been in vain. They would have had job descriptions that were impossible to fulfill. Frustration and confusion would have led them to abandon their posts.

Similarly, training disciples without establishing a strong regional structure through which they might be "built up" is an exercise in futility. We are called "living stones" and are admonished to be joined and fitted together (1 Peter 2:5; Ephesians 2:20-22). Although this command was never intended to be applied only at the local church level, it is rare that this concept is encouraged beyond the walls of individual churches.

If we begin to view local churches as "living stone conglomerates" (i.e. pillars, walls, and rooms) it will bring clarity to the imagery. There were many large components to Solomon's Temple that were impressive apart from the whole. Yet none of these parts disconnected from the whole were able to house God's presence.

Many powerful churches and ministries have "stand alone/all inclusive" status; nevertheless, they can never be "the whole." We hunger for glory to fall, but if Solomon haphazardly scattered stones and pillars throughout Israel and then begged for God to reveal His glory, it would be laughable.

There are limited opportunities for service at most churches. Even the largest and most active churches cannot always provide outreach opportunities that fully utilize the strengths and passions of every member. Without meaningful ministry, many saints succumb to an audience status. Even the greatest king of Israel fell prey to the temptations of an idle lifestyle. While his armies were at war, King David had balcony seats for a show that almost cost him the kingdom (2 Samuel 11). There are many churches in America that have over ten thousand members. They are larger than some small cities.

Wisely facilitating these amazing human resources is an incomprehensible endeavor. If we are able, however, to think regionally and send battalions of saints to assist struggling parish churches, we can accomplish two purposes: 1. The needs of a desperate community can be powerfully met, and 2. the need of our saints to be about the good work of the kingdom can be satisfied.

When ZIP codes, schools and housing projects are adopted and businessmen work together to create jobs and mentor floundering young men; when congregations are given the tools to join the fight against violence, drug trade and human trafficking; when prayer evangelism is a way of life, when every block has a neighborhood shepherd and the widow and orphan are being cared for, the saints will be strong and satisfied as they begin to walk in the fullness of their calling. The Lord's House will be full and flourishing.

Skeptics will say, "The saints are lazy." I may have had similar thoughts -- until I saw the tens of thousands of believers flooding my city after Superstorm Sandy. They out-flooded the ocean. It is their love that has been imprinted on the hearts of the flood victims, more so than the trauma of the storm.

Old men, young girls, housewives, teenagers, youth groups, and men's groups came, wave after wave. They gutted homes, they prayed with weeping strangers, they cleaned sewage off family pictures. They picked up sledge hammers and axes for the first time in their lives and worked until they had blisters. They cooked, cleaned, mopped, rebuilt, beautified, and blessed. They are still coming.

Our Church operates a six-week, full day summer camp. Every year, dozens of volunteers sleep on the floor of our church and serve about a hundred inner city children for one to two weeks. They often cry when they leave, as do the children they have so tenderly served. A father and his daughter told me that they enjoy serving at our summer camp more than going to Disney!

We gave them an opportunity to engage in meaningful, life-changing ministry, and they rose to the challenge. I truly believe that when our people see us operating in unity and seeking to saturate our cities and our world with the Gospel, each will find their place and be impassioned to be about the good work. There is a powerful army waiting for the call.

DISCUSSION QUESTIONS:

1. How solid and saturated of a "living stone" are you now?

2. What steps do you need to take to "return to your first love," be filled anew with God's Spirit and be rightly connected to your family and the body of Christ, local and regional?

3. Identify your own personal "Jerusalem", "Judea", "Samaria", and "Ends of the Earth.

4. Begin to pray for three people in each quadrant or circle. Then ask God to open doors for the sharing of the Gospel with them.

CHAPTER SEVEN

In Staten Island, I have experienced the evolution of a powerful, unified Church. But make no mistake; twenty years ago, it felt like civil war. Backbiting, jealousy, "sheep-stealing", gossip, division, betrayal, and even hatred were the norm. A particularly dark period of time when a pastor of a large church had a heart attack is cemented in my memory. As he lay in the hospital being prepared for a quadruple bypass, I bumped into another Staten Island pastor. His commentary was, "I guess that's what happens when you build your own kingdom."

Less than ten years ago, a small local church with about twenty members had a strong disagreement. It took years for the warring parties to resolve their differences. During those years, an enormous rift developed in Staten Island between churches that took sides with one party or the other. Churches and believers on both sides found it hard to fellowship during that time. I recall being bewildered at the devastating impact this tiny church could have on our borough of half a million.

Paul's appeal to Euodia and Syntche (Philippians 4:2) seems so trivial in light of the world-impacting message that Paul is constantly seeking to convey. Regardless, the Lord ordained that the names of these two arguing women be permanently etched into the Holy Scriptures. The truth that God is communicating is that there are no small divisions; they are all cataclysmic.

It was hard to do anything together in those days. Big "unity" events often led to more disunity because of political wrestling matches, inequitable burden sharing and the normal challenges of teamwork. As I look back, it is clear that city oneness began small and progressed slowly and relationally.

Our small pastor's association kept us connected. Over the years, trust was built and friendships were nurtured. Large and small prayer and worship initiatives began to bring splintered parties together. Slowly, but surely, brotherly love began to blossom.

We had become "friendly competitors." Then, a deep desire to honor John 17 arose. We began to see ourselves as "many tribes" but "one nation." This was truly the desire of many, but we were unsure what that looked like practically.

As I look back, it is clear that city oneness began small and progressed slowly and relationally.

We didn't know how to proceed from brotherly love to a unified body, from emotional unity to functional unity. We were less competitive and cloistered but still didn't have a good system of communication or a strategy for collaboration. This was much better than fighting, but still ineffective.

There is no question that the immense crisis that Superstorm Sandy brought to our shores created a "sink or swim" moment. Glenn Barth duly notes in his book, *The Good City*, that great community crisis is often the catalyst that catapults a city unity movement[1]. However, our experience told a different story.

Eight months after Sandy hit, the SIAE conducted our annual meeting. Many of us were excited about the remarkable fruit of our disaster response. The deep and powerful bonds engendered in the trenches seemed to set the stage for a powerful new era for the

---

1. Glenn Barth, *The Good City* (Tallmadge, OH: Good Place Publishing, 2010), 46.

Church of Staten Island. Yet to our dismay, the meeting got ugly and our war weary, exhausted coalition of churches was ready to throw in the towel and dissolve the association altogether. Personally, I was baffled beyond belief. We had just completed the most impactful season of unified ministry that our borough had ever experienced, but dissolution seemed inevitable. Tensions were inexplicably high. As I think about this meeting, it still perplexes me. Many of us were excited about the future prospects of our association, which seemed so bright. We had received numerous accolades and encouragements for our crisis response, yet on this crucial day, anger, cynicism, posturing, and old resentments filled air. No doubt, "Diabolos" was working the room.

The title of this chapter is "Sweet Hour of Prayer" because local church oneness is impossible apart from a miracle. In John 15, the Lord declares, "I am the vine and you are the branches, apart from me you can do nothing." Experience and the testimony of scripture seem to support the possibility that Christian unity endeavors may be the most challenging of all things. If we can't do anything apart from Christ, imagine taking on a church unity endeavor devoid of spiritual power.

We are awestruck when we read the book of Acts. Healings, resurrections, deliverance, signs and wonders fill every page. However, there is an unsung outpouring of God's Spirit without which the cumulative impact of every sign and wonder in the early Church would have been for naught: the miracle of oneness.

The most terrifying moment in the New Testament Church centers on unity as well. More terrifying than the martyrdom of Stephen and James is the theological division between Peter and Paul. Peter was the leader of the infant Church. Paul was, for many years, the untrusted outsider. If Peter had not received Paul's rebuke with a repentant and humble spirit, the fledgling New Testament Church could have experienced a devastating split (Galatians 2:11). There is no telling what the ramifications would have been. Collapse, disintegration or heretical splinter groups are a few of the potential tragic fruits.

There is also no other endeavor for which our Lord intercedes and cries out more passionately, than oneness in the Body of Christ. Throughout John 17, Jesus summons all the power of the Godhead on our behalf to enable us to walk in oneness. Christ Himself intercedes for this (vs. 9). He invokes the authority and protection of the Name of God for this cause on our behalf (vs. 6, 11, 12). He give us the glory that was given to Him by the Father (vs. 22) "in order that we might be one." He even proclaims the exciting, world transforming fruit of perfect oneness, "that the world may know that" the Father sent Jesus Christ (17:23). Jesus makes two things abundantly clear about Church unity: phenomenal power is available and phenomenal power is essential.

Our pastors' association had been in existence for more than twenty-five years. Our coalition had just served together side by side in the trenches for eight straight months. Thirty-year "disaster relief ministry" veterans told us they had never seen a better organized collaborative church disaster response. We had accomplished so much together, yet the end seemed inevitable. As a last ditch effort to "save the Bailey Building and Loan," we voted to press the pause button on dissolving the SIAE and devote the next year to meeting weekly for prayer.

It was June 2013. Historically, we suspended any and all of our sporadic monthly meetings for the summer, so the prospects of success for weekly prayer were slim to none. Yet each week of that summer, five to ten of us gathered for prayer. As fall rolled in, more came and sweet incense continued to rise to God's throne. The tensions and political wrestling that dominated our June meeting were forgotten in the presence of Jehovah. We prayed for each other, prayed for our city, prayed for the Church of Staten Island, prayed for revival throughout the earth. We prayed.

We felt God's favor on all sides. Wherever we put our feet, He gave us the land. We continued to rebuild storm-damaged homes. We continued to adopt housing projects. We were able to orchestrate several powerful outreaches in our local schools. Then the Luis Palau Association (LPA) came with a heart to bless our city. We secretly believed that it was our prayers that brought them (at least a little bit).

This is not an advertisement, but a true statement. Never in thirty years of ministry in NYC have I seen an organization work as hard as LPA did to bring together the body of Christ. They listened to, served, and engaged indigenous leadership for two years. They did not obsess about the big Central Park crusade as the crowning moment of two years of labor. Instead, they passionately endeavored to serve our city and strengthen collaborative ministry at the local level.

LPA richly blessed and strengthened our praying pastors. We felt the favor of God fall sweetly as LPA sponsored nearly a dozen powerful evangelistic outreaches in every corner of our borough. Thousands were reached and hundreds were saved in some of the neediest neighborhoods on Staten Island.

We have been praying together weekly for over two years now. We truly enjoy each other's company and seek to bless one another whenever possible. We don't have an exciting weekly agenda. No killer speakers, brilliant workshops or gourmet breakfasts. But we have found time and time again that the train of His robe encircles our gathering. We worship and pray.

It has become a way of life and a place of healing. Friendships are born and nurtured every week. We pray for and care for one another. Sometimes we cry on each other's shoulders in times of tragedy and sorrow. We do our best to bear together the unique burden of ministry.

The weekly connection enables constant dialogue about outreaches and initiatives. Whenever possible all or a few churches collaborate. At one point, around eight churches came alongside one church plant in a local housing project.

Another day as we sipped coffee and ate stale donuts, Pastor Chris Dito shared with us how successful his "Free Mother's Day Family Portrait" outreach was. He gladly shared his approach and the next Mother's Day or Easter Sunday, several churches did the same thing. At New Hope, we had the biggest crowd ever on Mother's Day. The attendees were dressed like they were going to a Broadway play. Every mom was overjoyed.

One winter I received a donation of five hundred beautiful coats. I gave out around seventy-five to the children in my community and church and shared the rest with all my friends who were adopting housing projects. Kids in the poorest neighborhoods of Staten Island were walking around with top-of-the-line Macy's winter coats.

When Pastor John Carlo received a donation of seventeen tons of Christian children's books, he put the word out to our coalition. By the end of the month, thousands of children throughout Staten Island were reading life-giving literature. These books help the children to call out to God in times of trouble. We hear stories from the parents all the time saying, "My son, he won't stop reading that book." "My daughter makes me read it to her every night." It brings us the greatest joy to know that these children, many of who don't attend a church, are learning to reach out to God from the youngest age.

In our own congregations, we speak well of and pray for other Staten Island churches. We rejoice when blessings fall on other pastors and their ministries. In the not-so-distant past, jealously and backbiting would often follow a great success story and tragedy often became the impetus for harsh criticism.

This is not to say there are not tensions and disagreements. It's just harder for divisive infections to fester and take root when there is consistent prayerful relationship. When our paths cross occasionally, it is easy to passively disconnect from those who offend us or those that we clash with. The sin of this becomes more apparent when it hinders us from praying together. As we gather to worship and intercede for our families and our city, foolishness of this sort quickly fades.

We are able to do large outreaches together now with no name lifted up but the name of Jesus. We even coordinate our calendars now for maximum synergy and kingdom impact. We are truly attempting to live out the Acts 1:8 strategic plan together to bless the heart of God and bring glory to His Name.

We feel that we have just begun to walk in a manner more pleasing to the Lord and more welcoming to His glory. It is encouraging to examine the testimony of scripture and history as we set our hearts in this direction.

In his excellent historical account of revivals, *The Concert of Prayer*, Brian Bakke reveals that nearly all of the great moves of God over the last two hundred years, came as the result of concerted interchurch prayer efforts.

The scriptural commands, stories and narratives are crystal clear. Where there is unity, there is glory. After the valley of dry bones came together, the Spirit filled the army. When the Temple and Tabernacle were completed, glory fell. When the disciples were gathered in one

place on Pentecost Sunday, holy fire filled the upper room. When two
or three are gathered in Christ's name, His presence is made manifest.
When hundreds and thousands walk as one man contending for the
faith, even greater glory falls.

A divided, disconnected, disjointed temple, army or body will
never experience the outpouring of God's authority and blessing that
we all hunger for. We have all experienced streams, but could there be
an ocean of glory that is being withheld until there is an obedient and
unified Church that can contain and honor it.

> I believe that in the same way that He was pierced for our transgressions and crushed for our iniquities, He was torn asunder to pay for and heal our division.

ALL MY BONES ARE OUT OF JOINT

In John 17 the appeal of Christ
for our oneness is almost desperate.
In Psalm 22, it is beyond desperate.
Here we enter into a soul-baring
prophetic revelation. A thousand
years before His crucifixion, we are
invited into the innermost chambers
of God's heart to hear the internal agony of Christ on the cross. "Dogs
encompass me...they have pierced my hands and my feet" (Psalm
22:16). "You lay me in the dust of death" (vs. 15). Then a cry seems to
echo across time from Golgotha's hill to every listening ear: "All my
bones are out of joint" (vs. 14).

I believe that in the same way that He was pierced for our trans-
gressions and crushed for our iniquities, He was torn asunder to pay
for and heal our division. As we ponder Christ's anguish as all His
bones were ripped out of joint, let our hearts be impassioned to bless
His heart and bring satisfaction to His soul as we His body come

together bone-to-bone and joint-to-joint. The choice of oneness is one of the deepest acts worship.

Just as we all sorrow when our own children are at war with one another; just as we are broken when our spouses are divided from us, God mourns over His divided body throughout the earth.

The impact of Church schisms in America alone is catastrophic. The power that binds us together can be compared to "atomic bonds." In learning how to break these bonds, mankind has unleashed the most devastating force known to man. Just as nuclear fallout destroys nations for generations, we are still reeling from the "North vs. South" denominational splits of the Methodists, Baptists and Presbyterians between 1844 and 1861. Many identify this ecclesiastical civil war as the beginning of the American Civil War in 1861.

The only force that we are aware of which is greater than nuclear fission or division is nuclear fusion. Fusion energy is the same energy that powers our sun and the stars.

Although we are still reeling from the sins and divisive inclinations of many of our forefathers, God is preparing to unleash a fusion powered revival through His Church in these last days. The Church in America is already an immense and mighty force for good. When our efforts are coordinated and collaborated, the collective impact will renew the face of the earth.

DISCUSSION QUESTIONS:

1. On a scale of 1-10, (1 being the least, 10 being the most); how well connected are the pastors in your region?

2. Using the same scale, how would you scale your commitment to seeing connection take place?

3. What are some creative ways churches near your own could co-labor for the Gospel and connect for the purposeful joining of the "living stones?"

4. How might you be used as a peacemaker in your city to reconcile warring pastors and churches?

5. Prayerfully consider starting or joining a pastor's prayer meeting in your area. Write down any hesitations that come to your mind and evaluate them in light of the previous chapter.

I began in ministry with a passion for social activism. I would often preach, "The first application of loving God was loving the least of these." I'm glad they didn't have podcasts back then to publicize my teetering on heresy. Heresy has been defined as "truth, out of balance." My imbalance nearly destroyed me and our young church. Through an excruciating period of soul renovation, God drew me near to Himself. By His grace I entered into the beautiful mystery of the Shema, seeking to "love the Lord my God with all my heart, soul, strength and mind." I learned the hard way that the first application of loving God was "loving God."

Sadly, however, I almost swung too far on the pendulum, away from the needs of the afflicted and broken that God had called me to serve. I unwittingly found myself embroiled in the age old Mary/ Martha dilemma. How tragic it is that to this day, worshippers and social activists still frustrate each other. Like Martha, the evangelists, disciple makers, and activists feel they are doing all the hard work, while the "Marys" (intercessors and worshippers) sing and pray around campfires "at the feet of Jesus." Whenever there is passion for one cause, there is often underlying disdain for another. This battle for priority has been a great stumbling block for ages.

I was recently was asked to teach a class on "Building a Citywide Prayer Movement." My opening comment at the workshop was, "I'd rather process with you the value of Building a Citywide Temple

Movement." I knew that my suggested title would not be the first one that pastors signed up for, so I didn't argue too fiercely to change it. Yet the truth is that for every compelling movement there is another valid and equally compelling one. Leaders are impassioned about numerous important Biblical issues and concerns. We need citywide movements for so many needs. Social justice, evangelism, prison ministry, discipleship, holiness, the presence of God, world missions, Jewish evangelism, friendship evangelism, community development; the list is long and too often divisive. How can we possibly divine "the most important thing?" Is there a sanctuary that can bless, house, and empower all holy and noble endeavors?

At this same conference, Dr. Eric Swanson spoke of the revolutionary business concept of building a "platform." In a recent blog he wrote: "a platform is an infrastructure that allows multiple participants (producers and consumers) to connect to it, interact with each other and create and exchange value. The world's largest taxi company, Uber, owns no vehicles. The world's most popular media owner, Facebook, creates no content...The world's largest accommodation provider, Airbnb, owns no real estate...Each of these companies have discovered the power of platforms to create value and serve customers." (http://ericjswanson.com/2015/08/platforms-and-city-transformation/)

He goes on to explore the potential that collaborative city movements have to provide a holy platform. As we dream like great commission contractors who are building a Holy Temple in our cities, the possibilities are astounding. No organization on earth is better engineered to provide cities with a unifying and healing platform. Despite all the challenges the Church faces, there is no other social structure that is better suited to "renew ruined cities" (Isa. 61:4). The Body of Christ in the U.S. alone boasts hundreds of thousands of

churches and millions of praying households and saints. Our potential is unfathomable.

When Uber decided to "evolve the way the world moves," nobody
believed that over 150,000 car owners would want to connect their
car to Uber's infrastructure. Is it possible that there are thousands
of Churches and millions of believers who long for a unifying infrastructure that is Christ centered, biblically grounded and passionate
to reach the lost? Our experience thus far is that this platform is wide
open and poised to expand like wildfire. There is a learning curve,
a kind of readjustment to a different mode of operation. Working
together is always challenging in the early stages but increasingly
beneficial over the long haul. We have found our collaboration is
becoming more fluid and impactful with each passing year.

In our work on Staten Island there has been no appreciable expen-
diture as we serve together. There is no facility and staff at this point,
just pastors, lay leaders and congregations working in harmony. We
have merely created a kind of platform based on Acts 1:8 and the
concept of building the New Covenant Temple together. This has
enabled us to work synergistically with dozens of different ministries and movements. It has enabled us to adopt dozens of zip codes,
schools and housing projects. It has enabled us to bring hundreds of
our young people together on a regular basis for encouragement and
mobilization. It has enabled us to launch transformational community outreach programs and bring relief to thousands of neighbors in
distress. Our unity has made it easier to work with principals, teachers, politicians, policemen and businessmen. Our little association of
pastors has become a nexus of sorts, a place where many good people
come together to do many good things and God causes His face to
shine upon us.

The building of the Temple and the Tabernacle similarly became the hub or nexus that brought the entire nation together. Each project incorporated the full scope of Israel's religious, political, civic and social structures. We see this clearly articulated in King David's final charge to complete the building of the Lord's House. Everyone in the nation was addressed, from Solomon to the peasants of Israel. Everyone from every walk and sector of society were welcomed to participate in the glorious work.

> David assembled at Jerusalem all the officials of Israel, the officials of the tribes, the officers of the divisions that served the king, the commanders of thousands, the commanders of hundreds, the stewards of all the property and livestock of the king and his sons, together with the palace officials, the mighty men and all the seasoned warriors. 2 Then King David rose to his feet and said: "Hear me, my brothers and my people. I had it in my heart to build a house of rest for the ark of the covenant of the Lord and for the footstool of our God, and I made preparations for building... 21... behold the divisions of the priests and the Levites for all the service of the house of God; and with you in all the work will be every willing man who has skill for any kind of service; also the officers and all the people will be wholly at your command."
> 1 Chronicles 28:1, 2, 21

In an article on cross-sector collaboration, Glenn Barth unpacks Moses' similarly comprehensive project.

"In Exodus 36-39 we read about the skilled workers who came together to build the Tabernacle under the leadership of Bezalel and Oholiab. There were workers in art, embroidery, woodworking, carpenters, metal fabricators and sculptors, priests, Levites, and people who gave great quantities of silver and gold (which at some point involved mining). There was acacia wood from the forests, animal skins from keepers of livestock, farmers who provided the first grain offerings, musicians, scribes, accountants, and many others who came together to create this center of worship and education" (Glenn Barth, 2014, *Whole Church, Whole City*, p.2,3).

In our context we welcome tutors, mentors, reading buddies, counselors, athletes, lawyers, contractors, volunteers, artists, politicians, community activists, children, retirees, intercessors, biblical scholars, gardeners, landscapers, farmers, nutritionists: "...every willing man (and woman), who has skill for any kind of service" (I Chronicles 28:21).

As we provide a Biblically based collaborative model that welcomes vast participation while creating tremendous synergy, there is constant blossoming. As we embrace our identity as a "Kingdom of Priests" building together the Lord's House, a powerful platform and unifying principle unfolds. We now see the ease at which the entirety of our calling can be encompassed in one holy house.

There is a song that we sing every anniversary of our church (and often in between) called: "A House of Hope." It's a kind of motto and dream we carry in our heart.

House of Hope

Gonna build a house, here on my block
Gonna set it down on a solid rock
A house of hope, in a world of pain
Where love is law and Jesus reigns

It's a house of hope In a world of pain
Talking 'bout a shelter from the driving rain
A place of peace in a world of fear
Where the hands of my Savior wipe away every tear

Gonna light a fire here on my street
Gonna let it shine with joy so sweet
A light of love, burning warm and strong
Breaking out in the darkness, till the new day dawns

Gonna build a fountain here on my land
Gonna let it flow through the burning sand
Gonna tell the children, rejoice and sing
Celebrate the glory of the King of Kings

I cannot let go of the dream that many of us sang in our youth: "Do you feel the darkness tremble, when all the saints join in one song and all the streams flow as one river, to wash away our brokenness." (Martin Smith, Delirious, "Did You Feel the Mountains Tremble"). We have all been called to dream Holy dreams. To join our visions, passions and faith with the dreams of God.

In a recent Charlie Rose interview, Josh Tyrangiel, the editor of Bloomberg Weekly, spoke of his behind-the-scenes experience at Apple's design studio. I found one of his statements fascinating. It was as if he had discovered the secret at the heart of this corporation: "There is a method to the way that Apple operates that is very unique – it is faith-based...they place more trust in their designers than we ever knew. It really is faith in designers and engineers."

For decades, this company has dazzled us with some of the most fascinating and innovative consumer products of the century. This is a corporation led by dreamers. Yet their faith and their dreams are earth-bound and profit-motivated. What is the potential latent in the Church if we were to faithfully dream the holy dreams planted in our souls by the King of Glory? We are those who are called to dream of the healing of communities, cities and nations. We must lead the world with holy dreams.

As we dream of our Fathers house, we begin to see in faith, all the streams flowing as one river. We begin to see in faith His house of hope filling and healing our world of pain. The Father's House endlessly radiates with His loving presence. His house is filled with ceaseless worship, praise and intercession. It is a house of salvation where all who call on the name of Jesus may enter and be saved. It is a house of rescue from which we are called to go to the highways and byways to compel the lost and broken to enter. It is a house of discipleship, where the living stones and priests learn of Christ face-to-face. It is a house of holiness where "holy to the Lord" is engraved upon our foreheads. It is the house of shalom, where peace flows like a river and "righteousness like an ever-flowing stream" (Amos 5:24).

The Lord's house is a shelter for the homeless and a healing sanctuary for the afflicted. Prodigals come home to open arms of love. The abused and the oppressed find compassion and justice there. There is always bread for the hungry and water for the thirsty.

In the Lord's house, iron sharpens iron as every saint's unique passion and gifting reveals another wondrous facet of God's glory. Here, an evangelistic/activist fire can be stirred up in the hearts of true worshippers, and the tenderness of intimacy with Christ is infused into the hearts of diehard evangelists and missionaries. In the Lord's House, megachurches and parish churches can walk as "one man contending for the faith." In the Lord's house, the carpenter who frames new Sunday school rooms, the gardener who helps the neighborhood children plant a community garden, and the soloist on the worship team can all rejoice in their high and holy calling.

All the tribes of Israel gathered several times a year at the Temple. Just as the matriarch of a family can bring warring brothers to the same table, our great Savior calls us to dine together. As a community based and built upon lavish grace, we must lead the world in reconciliation by starting in our own house. Like the great celebration of Jubilee, churches, denominations, ministries and movements can forgive historic grievances and pursue the liberation of all captives.

The word of God speaks of a holy flood that will flow from the

Temple at the consummation of the ages. Wherever this river flows, it brings life. Trees flourish on the banks of this river and their leaves bring healing to the nations (Ezekiel 47:1-12; Rev. 22:2). Even now, from the Temple that God has built in our hearts, from every regional Church and from THE Church international, rivers of living water are flowing, flooding and saturating barren and broken lands. Our Lord is calling for all these mighty streams and rivers to flow as one. Just as the trauma of Hurricane Sandy was catalytic for a new era of unity in our city, the rising flood of evil throughout the world is bringing about a new era of true and holy oneness.

A holy, healing, glorious saturating river is rising. A holy, healing, glorious earth encompassing Temple is coming together. It is to this Temple that people will flow from every tribe, tongue and nation (Isaiah 2:3; Micah 4:2). In ever-increasing measure, the Lord's House and the knowledge of His glory will cover the earth as the water covers the sea (Habakkuk 2:14).

ABOUT THE AUTHOR

Rev. David Beidel has lived in Staten Island, NY, for most of his life. In 1990, he and his wife, Rebecca, started a church in their home in New Brighton, a crime-ridden community in Staten Island. Twenty-three years later, New Hope Community Church stands as a beacon of hope among the West Brighton Housing Projects on the north shore of Staten Island, where David and Rebecca continue to serve that community faithfully.

Rev. Beidel spearheads the SIAE Acts 1:8 "Saturate" initiative. This collaborative strategic approach facilitates strategic regional ministry to: Jerusalem" (zip codes), "Judea" (Public Schools), "Samaria" (NYC Housing Projects) and "the ends of the earth" (local ethnic enclaves).

In addition to his role as pastor/teacher, David is an anointed psalmist and guitarist, having penned numerous songs of worship. Many of his songs have been recorded on three worship albums featuring New Hope's worship team: Fragrance, A Pleasing Offering and Magnificent Obsession.

In addition to his heart for the broken in NYC, God's heart for the nations has taken root in Pastor Dave's heart as well. He has ministered in Central Asia, Nigeria and Hyderabad, India where New Hope has planted a daughter church. Driven by God's promises in Isaiah 35, Pastor Dave longs to see "the desert and the parched lands" of New York City and the ends of the earth flowing with streams of Living Water.

David and Rebecca and their four children, Julianne, David, Emily, and Caleb, live in Staten Island's West Brighton neighborhood.

Made in the USA
Columbia, SC
15 March 2020